NEWCASTLE UNITED

THE OFFICIAL
NEWCASTLE UNITED

ANNUAL 2010

**WRITTEN BY
MARK HANNEN**

**CONTRIBUTIONS FROM
DAN SHERIDAN, PAUL TULLY,
DAN KING, TIM BARTON
AND GAV GRIEVES**

A Grange Publication

© 2009. Published by Grange Communications Ltd., Edinburgh,
under licence from Newcastle United Football Club.

Printed in the EU.

Every effort has been made to ensure the accuracy of information
within this publication but the publishers cannot be held responsible
for any errors or omissions. Views expressed are those of the author
and do not necessarily represent those of the publishers or
the football club. All rights reserved.

Photographs © Newcastle United Football Club.

Thanks to Paul Joannou.

Photography by Ian Horrocks and Serena Taylor.

ISBN 978-1-906211-84-4

£6.99

CONTENTS

NEWCASTLE UNITED

WELCOME TO THE NEWCASTLE UNITED ANNUAL 2010

UNITED ARE A CLUB WITH A REMARKABLE HISTORY AND ALTHOUGH THE MAGPIES KICKED OFF THE 2009/10 CAMPAIGN IN THE COCA-COLA CHAMPIONSHIP, THERE IS NO DOUBTING THE FINE TRADITION THE CLUB HAS, HAVING ENJOYED MANY GLORIOUS MOMENTS DURING ITS 118-YEAR HISTORY.

A club with fervent and loyal support, with a Champions League pedigree only a few short years ago, Newcastle United is potentially one of the biggest clubs in Europe, playing in a magnificently redeveloped 52,387 capacity St. James' Park – the third highest capacity amongst club stadiums in England.

Dwelling on the past is all well and good but it's today that matters and it is everyone's burning desire at St. James' Park to see United back in the Premier League come the end of this season.

It may well be a roller-coaster ride, so hang on tight. We hope it's an enjoyable, but above all, successful season for black n' whites throughout the world.

A SEASON OF STRUGGLE

THE GOING WAS NEVER EASY IN 2008-09 AND RELEGATION WAS THE FINAL FATE.

UNITED OPEN THE SEASON WITH A POINT AT OLD TRAFFORD

AUGUST 2008

IN FRONT OF 75,512 SPECTATORS AT THE THEATRE OF DREAMS, OBA MARTINS' FIRST-HALF HEADER THREATENED TO INFLICT FIRST-DAY DEFEAT ON THE CHAMPIONS, AND EVEN THOUGH DARREN FLETCHER'S GOAL DIVIDED THE POINTS, THIS WAS A TRULY ENCOURAGING START FOR THE MAGPIES.

The positive start carried on into the next game, when Shay Given's dramatic penalty save from Kevin Nolan laid the foundation for a victory sealed by a late Michael Owen header.

Captain Owen was on target again in the 3-2 extra-time Carling Cup win at Coventry, though the Sky Blues came back from two down to level deep into injury time.

However, United's undefeated start was firmly shattered and reality dawned when Arsenal hammered in three goals without reply at The Emirates Stadium, two of them from Robin van Persie, at the end of the month.

SEPTEMBER 2008

MANAGER KEVIN KEEGAN PARTED COMPANY WITH THE CLUB BEFORE PREMIER LEAGUE NEWCOMERS HULL CITY CONTINUED THEIR EXCELLENT START TO THE SEASON BY WINNING 2-1 AT ST. JAMES', MARLON KING SCORING TWICE BEFORE A LATE XISCO REPLY.

Chris Hughton took temporary charge as United went down 3-1 at West Ham after a brace from David Di Michele, and a Carling Cup home exit at the hands of holders Tottenham Hotspur when another consolation goal came from Michael Owen.

After the 2-1 home defeat by Blackburn Rovers, Joe Kinnear was drafted in to turn a sad September into an optimistic October.

OCTOBER 2008

AND WHAT A FINE START KINNEAR ENJOYED. IN HIS FIRST GAME, AT EVERTON, IT LOOKED LIKE SAME AGAIN AS MIKEL ARTETA AND MAROUANE FELLAINI PUT THE TOFFEES TWO AHEAD, BUT SECONDS BEFORE HALF-TIME STEVEN TAYLOR PULLED ONE GOAL BACK AND MOMENTS AFTER THE BREAK DAMIEN DUFF EQUALISED.

With Manchester City the opposition for Kinnear's first home game, hopes were high, though when Habib Beye was wrongly sent off for a good tackle on Robinho, who converted the penalty, United were up against it.

Remarkably, Shola Ameobi equalised, and a Richard Dunne own goal looked set to bring full points – until Stephen Ireland snatched an 88th-minute City equaliser.

Consequent defeat in the big derby at Sunderland – Ameobi again scored but Kieran Richardson's explosive free-kick cost United defeat – was followed by two successive home wins over Midland opposition which brightened the picture.

Joey Barton and Oba Martins despatched West Bromwich to a 2-1 loss, and six days later resurgent Aston Villa came to Tyneside.

SHOLA AMEOBI EQUALISES AT THE STADIUM OF LIGHT

IN ARGUABLY THE FINEST DISPLAY OF THE SEASON UNITED SUNK MARTIN O'NEILL'S VILLA WITH TWO SECOND-HALF STRIKES FROM OBA MARTINS TO CAP A FIRST-CLASS TEAM PERFORMANCE.

United took their improved form to improved Fulham, who got the better of United at Craven Cottage with a Danny Murphy penalty after Shola Ameobi had equalised Andy Johnson's opener.

That meant United needed three points against Wigan at St. James' Park to get back on track, and when Michael Owen and Oba Martins each scored in the final ten minutes to put United 2-1 up, three points looked certain. But old boy Titus Bramble made it late heartbreak with a headed equaliser.

United had failed to scored only once in the first 15 games and had avoided conceding only twice, but in successive games away to Chelsea and Middlesbrough it was 0-0 – two decent away results which gave sight of a new-style United under Kinnear.

STALEMATE AT STAMFORD BRIDGE

OBA MARTINS FINDS THE BACK OF THE VILLA NET

DECEMBER 2008

ONCE AGAIN, THE LAUNCHING-PAD WAS THERE FOR UNITED AS THEY TOOK ON PREMIER LEAGUE NEW BOYS STOKE CITY AT ST. JAMES', AND WHEN MICHAEL OWEN PLANTED TWO GOALS INTO THE POTTERS' NET IN THE FIRST 24 MINUTES, IT LOOKED A SURE HOME VICTORY. IT ALL FELL APART, THOUGH, WHEN MAMADY SIDIBE HALVED THE DEFICIT ON THE HOUR… AND FORMER UNITED DEFENDER ABDOULAYE FAYE FIRED IN AN INJURY-TIME EQUALISER.

For the second time in the season, however, United responded to major disappointment with a pair of victories. Birthday boy Michael Owen, followed by Oba Martins and Danny Guthrie, hit the second-half goals that destroyed Tony Adams' Portsmouth at Fratton Park to bring up the biggest win of the season.

Seven days later, it was Sunday Best again for Kinnear and his merry men as Damien Duff rolled in a last-minute winner at the Leazes End to bury Spurs.

Yet 2008 was destined to go out on a low note, with Wigan winning the Boxing Day meeting at the JJB 2-1, and Liverpool turning on all their power to race to a 5-1 triumph at St. James'.

MICHAEL OWEN HITS UNITED'S FIRST AGAINST THE HAMMERS

JANUARY 2009

COMETH THE NEW YEAR, COMETH THE FA CUP. AND THE LUCK OF THE DRAW SENT UNITED TO HUMBERSIDE TO FACE A HULL SIDE LOSING IMPETUS SINCE THEIR BRIGHT OPENING.

Goalless at the KC Stadium, City took the replay at St. James' 1-0 with a late Daniel Cousin goal. Between the two Cup games, United were held 2-2 at home by West Ham, though when Craig Bellamy and Carlton Cole put West Ham ahead 2-1 they needed a saviour – and local boy Andy Carroll obliged with a late header that earned a point.

United were in a season's-best 11th place then, but Sam Allardyce's Blackburn dumped United 3-0 at Ewood Park and Wednesday night defeat at Manchester City, and another bad injury to Joey Barton, meant United were sliding down the table.

FEBRUARY 2009

THE 1-1 DERBY DRAW AT HOME TO SUNDERLAND – SHOLA AMEOBI'S PENALTY EQUALISING DJIBRIL CISSE'S OPENER - SCARCELY IMPROVED MATTERS, AND THE FEBRUARY 7TH TRIP TO BOTTOM CLUB WEST BROMWICH THUS TOOK ON EXTRA MEANING

In a hectic opening nine minutes at The Hawthorns Damien Duff and Peter Lovenkrands gave United a 2-1 lead. Steven Taylor's header made it 3-1 by half-time and a second goal from Marc-Antoine Fortune could not deny United three points.

However, Kinnear, taken ill in the team hotel on the morning of the match, spent the day in hospital and would thereafter take no direct part in team affairs for the rest of the campaign. Chris Hughton again assumed control.

There was a three-week wait until the next game, a goalless home draw with Everton in which Kevin Nolan was sent off for a challenge on Victor Anichebe.

DAMIEN DUFF GIVES UNITED A DREAM START AT THE HAWTHORNS

AS THE RELEGATION FIGHT GREW, BOLTON PULLED OFF A VITAL WIN WITH RICARDO GARDNER'S STRIKE THE ONLY GOAL OF THE GAME AT THE REEBOK STADIUM.

To follow was another dastardly deed of the fixture computer – three successive home matches against Manchester United, Arsenal and Chelsea, with only a trip to Hull to split them up.

Peter Lovenkrands ended Edwin van der Sar's long, long spell without conceding a goal, and for a time the Magpies looked good for a dividend against the Red Devils – but Wayne Rooney equalised on 20 minutes and 11 minutes into the second half Dimitar Berbatov hit the winner after a Ryan Taylor error.

Steven Taylor's volley earned a point at Hull to set up the Arsenal game, and when Oba Martins fired home within a minute of Nicklas Bendtner's opener for Arsenal, the St. James' faithful envisaged reward... but the Gunners responded with quickfire strikes from Abou Diaby and Samir Nasri to make it a top-team double on Tyneside.

THE RED DEVILS ARE STUNNED
BY PETER LOVENKRANDS' OPENER

APRIL 2009

NOW THE PRESSURE WAS TRULY ON – AND UNITED'S HIERARCHY ACTED DECISIVELY BY BRINGING IN GEORDIE IDOL ALAN SHEARER AS MANAGER THREE YEARS AFTER HE LAST KICKED A BALL. IT WAS IN AT THE DEEP END FOR ALAN – FOR CHELSEA CAME, SAW AND CONQUERED WITH FRANK LAMPARD AND FLORENT MALOUDA ON TARGET TO SILENCE THE GEORDIE CROWD AND MAKE IT A TOP-TEAM TREBLE.

That made the Potteries clash with Stoke a six-pointer, and when Abdoulaye Faye headed home a corner after 33 minutes it looked bad for United... until substitute Andy Carroll headed in Damien Duff's cross for a late equaliser.

The launching-pad? Well, Spurs had other ideas as Darren Bent struck the only goal of the game at White Hart Lane.

And when April ended with a tense goalless draw at home to Portsmouth, United were left three points adrift of safety with just four games remaining.

MAY 2009

TITLE-CHASING LIVERPOOL HAD INFLICTED UNITED'S HEAVIEST DEFEAT OF THE SEASON, 5-1 AT ST. JAMES' PARK IN DECEMBER, AND THEY MATCHED THE HEAVIEST AWAY DEFEAT WITH A 3-0 VICTORY AT ANFIELD TO BEGIN THE SEASON'S FINAL MONTH. YOSSI BENAYOUN, DIRK KUYT AND LUCAS WERE THE MARKSMEN – AND THE SENDING-OFF OF JOEY BARTON FOR A TACKLE ON XABI ALONSO 13 MINUTES FROM TIME ADDED INSULT TO INJURY.

By the time Middlesbrough came to call in the penultimate home match, United were third from bottom, three points adrift of Hull City. But after Hull's home defeat by Stoke, United turned on the style in the Tyne-Tees derby, recovering from an early Habib Beye own goal to triumph through strikes from Steven Taylor, Oba Martins – within 55 seconds of replacing Michael Owen – and finally Peter Lovenkrands.

That lifted the entire camp... but five days later Fulham, strong European candidates with a formidable defensive record, shut out United and poached the only goal – arguably offside – through Diomansy Kamara, and survived an apparently legitimate Mark Viduka equaliser, ruled out by referee Howard Webb for a foul by Kevin Nolan that even TV replays scarcely corroborated.

And so, with United back in the bottom three, everything was left riding on the final-day trip to Aston Villa, while Hull City and Sunderland faced tricky home games against Manchester United and Chelsea.

Hopes were heightened with a bright start in which Steven Taylor, Damien Duff and Oba Martins all went close.

Then, when news came through that Hull City were trailing to Manchester United, the route through the escape tunnel widened even further.

But eight minutes before half-time the cruel fortune that has afflicted United all season struck again as Gareth Barry's wayward shot took a wicked deflection off the covering Duff and wrong-footed Steve Harper on its way into the bottom left corner. That gave Villa the boost they needed and they were largely in control of the second half as the tension grew to breaking point.

Hull lost, and Sunderland lost. But United were unable to grab the single goal they needed to stave off relegation, and when a late, late Jose Enrique shot slipped wide, United's final hopes slipped away with it.

STEVEN TAYLOR POWERS HOME A HEADER AGAINST MIDDLESBROUGH

QUIZ 1.

WHAT DO YOU REMEMBER ABOUT THE 2008/09 SEASON?

1 WHO SCORED UNITED'S FIRST AND LAST PREMIER LEAGUE GOALS OF THE SEASON?

2 WHO KNOCKED UNITED OUT OF THE LEAGUE CUP COMPETITION?

3 WHICH FORMER UNITED PLAYER SCORED AGAINST THE MAGPIES AT EASTLANDS?

4 WHICH TEAM DID UNITED SIGN DANNY GUTHRIE FROM?

5 WHERE DID YOUNG STRIKER KAZENGA LUALUA SPEND THE LAST PART OF THE SEASON ON LOAN?

6 WHO WAS THE ONLY UNITED PLAYER TO SCORE IN THE TWO TYNE/WEAR DERBY MATCHES?

7 WHICH TEAM DID UNITED DO THE 'LEAGUE DOUBLE' OVER?

8 WHICH WAS THE ONLY GROUND NEWCASTLE UNITED PLAYED TWO MATCHES AT LAST SEASON?

9 WHO MISSED A PENALTY FOR BOLTON WHEN UNITED BEAT THEM AT THE START OF THE SEASON?

10 WHICH CURRENT UNITED PLAYER SCORED AGAINST NEWCASTLE IN 2007/08?

ANSWERS PAGE 61

CLASSIC CLASHES

NEWCASTLE UNITED HAVE BEEN INVOLVED IN MANY MEMORABLE AND OUTSTANDING MATCHES IN THEIR HISTORY. SOME ARE LABELLED 'GREAT' BECAUSE OF THE EXCITEMENT GENERATED, SOME BY THEIR SIGNIFICANCE AND SOME BY THE TERRIFIC FOOTBALL PLAYED AND QUALITY OF THE GOALS SCORED.

GAMES SUCH AS THE 5 – 0 HAMMERING OF MANCHESTER UNITED IN 1996 AND THE 3 – 2 DEFEAT OF BARCELONA IN 1997 HAVE BEEN CHRONICLED MANY TIMES OVER SO ON THIS OCCASION, THOSE GAMES ARE NOT INCLUDED

INSTEAD WE'VE SELECTED THREE OTHER GAMES FROM THE FAIRLY RECENT PAST AND OUTLINE JUST WHY THEY WILL ALWAYS STICK IN THE MEMORY OF UNITED FANS.

BRUCE GROBBELAAR IS HELPLESS AGAINST GOAL KING COLE

09 MAY 1993

FOOTBALL LEAGUE DIVISION ONE
NEWCASTLE 7 - 1 LEICESTER CITY

What a way to end United's victorious Championship winning season. Promotion had been clinched on a glorious night at Grimsby five days earlier and the Championship wrapped up two days later at home to Oxford. But this was the real celebration match. The Foxes, only six places behind United in the table, were the Gallowgate sacrificial lambs.

Brian Kilcline and Barry Venison had received the Championship Trophies before the game and in a carnival atmosphere, United played rip-roaring thrilling football and were an incredible six goals in front after the first 45 minutes. David Kelly claimed a 17-minute hat-trick after Andy Cole had opened the scoring on 5 minutes. Cole and Lee made it the round half dozen in the five minutes before the break and Cole completed his hat-trick on 66 minutes. The crowd scenes were incredible as the 'Andy Cole' song reverberated around all four sides of the ground.

In many ways the second half couldn't have been anything else other than an anti-climax and Steve Walsh's goal eight minutes from time was the merest of consolations.

The Premier League had been warned, United were on their way.

UNITED. SRNICEK, VENISON, BERESFORD (PEACOCK), ROBINSON, SCOTT, HOWEY (KILCLINE), LEE, COLE, KELLY, CLARK, SELLARS. SCORERS. COLE 5, 40, 66, LEE 13, KELLY 28, 34, 45.

21 NOVEMBER 1993

PREMIERSHIP
NEWCASTLE 3 - 0 LIVERPOOL

United had won their previous two games spectacularly against Wimbledon and Oldham, to continue their climb up the Premier League in this their first season back in the big-time. Merseyside giants Liverpool, occupying fifth place in the league, four places higher than United, were stern opposition but in a game played out in front of millions on Sky Television, the Magpies, and Andy Cole in particular, illuminated the dark Tyneside skies. Ahead on 4 minutes, and three up by the half-hour, United had produced a scintillating display of attacking football to pummel the Scousers into submission.

Snow was falling, the pitch was slippy but that didn't stop the Magpies running riot as goal-machine Andy Cole put the Reds' defence to the sword with three predatory strikes, all of which whistled past a helpless and bemused Bruce Grobbelaar at the Gallowgate End.

Anfield goal-scoring legends Ian Rush and Robbie Fowler barely got a kick, Kevin Scott and Steve Watson at the heart of the United back four providing a formidable barrier.

UNITED. HOOPER, WATSON, ELLIOTT, VENISON, SCOTT BRACEWELL, LEE, CLARK, COLE, BEARDSLEY, SELLARS SCORERS. COLE 4, 15, 30

02 FEBRUARY 1997

PREMIERSHIP
NEWCASTLE 4 - 3 LEICESTER CITY

Barely four weeks had passed since Kevin Keegan had left United and Kenny Dalglish had assumed control but, the Magpies had maintained their fourth place in the League in a season that ultimately saw the Black and Whites finish in second place and with that gain, a Champions League spot the following season. And it was results like this, incredible as they were, which helped propel United up the table.

Robbie Elliott put United one up as early as the third minute and things were looking good for a fourth successive home win until the Foxes hit United with three goals in a 14-minute either side of the hour mark. Shell-shocked United didn't know what had hit them but Alan Shearer, in his first season at Gallowgate, came up trumps with the first hat-trick of his United career to send a devastated Leicester side back home to the Midlands pointless.

The first arrived on 77 minutes with a cross shot that found its way through a crowded box into the corner of the Gallowgate net, the second was a howitzer of a free kick six minutes later that Kasey Keller could only wave at as it smashed into the net and the winner, right at the death, in front of an increasingly frenzied support, came as Rob Lee and substitute Lee Clark combined down the right for the latter to cross into the six-yard box where Shearer bundled the ball into the net. A truly amazing finish.

UNITED. **HISLOP; WATSON, ELLIOTT, PEACOCK, ALBERT, BATTY, ASPRILLA (CLARK), LEE, SHEARER, FERDINAND, GILLESPIE (GINOLA).** SCORERS. **ELLIOTT 3, SHEARER 77, 83, 90.**

STADIUM PROFILE

ST JAMES' PARK BOASTS THE FOURTH HIGHEST CAPACITY IN BRITISH CLUB FOOTBALL. IT HAS SEEN FOOTBALL PLAYED ON ITS HALLOWED TURF FOR NEARLY 130 YEARS! IT WAS WAY BACK IN 1880 THAT NEWCASTLE RANGERS FIRST USED THE GROUND WHICH LEGENDS SUCH AS GALLACHER, MILBURN AND SHEARER WOULD GRACE IN THE YEARS TO COME. THERE HAVE BEEN MANY MILESTONES TO NOTE OVER THE YEARS. HERE ARE JUST A FEW.

1880 First game of football; Newcastle Rangers practice match.

1886 Newcastle West End take up residence.

1889 Wooden boards laid as terracing.

1892 Newcastle East End (Newcastle United) take over the lease.

1899 Major development work undertaken; capacity set at 30,000.

1905 Complete redevelopment takes place increasing the capacity to over 60,000.

1926 Stands planned on the open terracing.

1930 Leazes End terrace roof erected behind the north goal and the picture opposite top illustrates how the ground would look look for the next four decades. The picture also shows the Popular Side east terrace and Gallowgate End open to the elements along with the West Stand paddock in front of the 1905 Grandstand.

1953 Floodlights used for the first time against Glasgow Celtic.

1959 An 80,000 capacity new plan is scrapped after failure to agree proposals.

1963 Redevelopment blocked and the World Cup matches are lost to Ayresome Park.

1967 Shared operation with the council and university dismissed by United.

1971 Overall development plan approved by the planning department.

1973 The Leazes Terrace stand – the East Stand – constructed. For five years the ground looked like this picture opposite middle, with the east and west stands flanking the Leazes End terrace roof. The Gallowgate End remained uncovered. The other difference between the two pictures of course is the floodlights.

1978 United's kop, the Leazes End is demolished.

1988 The Edwardian West Stand is condemned and the Milburn Stand is built in its place.

1993 The Sir John Hall Stand at Leazes is opened.

1994 The Gallowgate Stand is constructed.

1995 Redevelopment plans for an all-seater stadium completed at a capacity of 36,518.

1997 United plan a new 65,000 stadium at Castle Leazes, but fail to win permission.

2000 St. James' Park increased in capacity to over 52,000 by enlarging the Milburn and Leazes stands.

CAPACITY
Sir John Hall Stand. 20,145
Milburn Stand. 14,929
Newcastle Brown Stand. 12,043
East Stand. 5,240
Television Podiums. 30
Total. 52,387

DISABLED ALLOWANCE
Meets the Green Guide Requirements and agreed with Disabled Access Group. Currently 187 wheelchair spaces in the stadium.

FAMILY AREA SEATS & EXECUTIVE BOXES
Family Area Seats. 5000
Executive Boxes. 82

CONFERENCE & BANQUETING FACILITIES
Catering for 4,500 in many varied size rooms and is now the largest in the North East. There are 82 Executive boxes within the stadium.

MATCHDAY
4500 meals, over 10,000 teas/coffees are served, 5,000 pies/chips, 30 cases of Newcastle Brown Ale, 500 bottles of wine, 200 bottles of champagne and around 800 staff.

CAR PARKING
Two multi-storey car parks adjacent/attached to stadium.

LENGTH OF CANTILEVER ROOF
65.5m (one of the largest in the world).
The distance from the highest seat to the pitch is 69m.
The commentary gantry is 20m high.

'SIZE' OF STADIUM
As the stadium is three different heights we use measurements for the pitch side including the track and average for the height - 123m x 81m x50m average height = 498,150 m3. Size of TV Gantry is 21m x 2.6m and TV Village 32m x 40m.

OTHER INFO
Floodlights. 66 on East Stand; 102 on Milburn Stand
Steel Tonnage. 7000 tonnes
Transparent Roof. 16200 sq. metres
Piles. 600 Concrete ground piles 15m deep
Height of roof from pitch. 41m
Height of rear seats above pitch. 39m
Height to top of roof truss mast. 60m

CAPACITY PROGRESSION

1882-1898	10,000-18,000	1990	33,530
1899-1905	30,000	1992	30,348
1905-1969	52,000-70,000	1993	36,931
1969-1973	61,500	1994	34,390
1973-1978	54,500	1995	36,518
1978	46,000	1996	36,610
1979	40,480	1998	36,834
1980	38,008	2000	52,193
1985	36,581		

FA CUP & LEAGUE CUP REVIEW

UNITED GO TO HULL AND BACK

RD 3. HULL CITY 0 - 0 NEWCASTLE UNITED
REPLAY. NEWCASTLE UNITED 0 - 1 HULL CITY

In the year marking the 40th anniversary of Newcastle's last Cup success – when Joe Harvey's boys won the Inter-Cities Fairs Cup in 1969 – United were desperate to bring some long-awaited silverware to Tyneside. But their FA Cup hopes were ended at the very first hurdle, albeit after a replay.

The Magpies came into the competition at the third round stage and were handed a very tough tie against a Hull City side who, at that stage, were still in the top half of the Barclays Premier League. And to make matters worse, Joe Kinnear had a handful of his key players missing at the KC Stadium. But United played well with Andy Carroll, making his first start of the season, posing a threat up front.

And although it was Hull who came closest to scoring, when Michael Turner's header hit the underside of post and bar before bouncing into the grateful arms of Shay Given, a 0-0 draw was a good result in the circumstances.

However, in the replay at a rainy St. James' Park 11 days later, United were unable to see the job through. They created more than enough chances to win the game but failed to find a way past City stopper Matt Duke – or the woodwork, as Nicky Butt saw a header crash against the bar – and with ten minutes left to play, Hull punished their prolifigacy. Bernard Mendy crossed and Daniel Cousin was on hand to turn the ball home and ensure that Newcastle were destined to end another season without a major trophy.

NICKY BUTT HEADS AGAINST THE BAR
IN THE GALLOWGATE REPLAY

MICHAEL OWEN WINS IT FOR UNITED AT THE RICOH

HOLDERS KNOCK OUT UNITED

RD 3. COVENTRY CITY 2 - 3 NEWCASTLE UNITED (AET)
REPLAY. NEWCASTLE UNITED 1 - 2 TOTTENHAM HOTSPUR

Newcastle had already drawn with champions Manchester United and beaten Bolton, and they continued their good start to the season in the Carling Cup by knocking out Coventry City... although they were given a scare by Chris Coleman's Sky Blues.

In what turned out be Kevin Keegan's penultimate game as manager, United surged into a two-goal lead through Charles N'Zogbia and James Milner at the Ricoh Arena. Jonás Gutiérrez played in Milner to cross from the left hand side of the penalty area and N'Zogbia got a touch just ahead of two Coventry defenders, then Milner doubled the lead with a cross-cum-shot shortly before half-time.

However, in first-half stoppage time a goal out of nothing from Clinton Morrison brought the home side back into the game and then in the dying seconds of the second half, a long, long throw from Aron Gunnarsson was headed in by Scott Dann. Fortunately in extra time, Michael Owen raced through to score the decisive goal.

Newcastle's reward was a home tie against Tottenham, the holders. After an uneventful first-half, Roman Pavlyuchenko scored for the North Londoners and four minutes later, Jamie O'Hara seized on an error from Steven Taylor before slotting home.

Michael Owen sparked hopes of a late comeback, tucking home from close range in the 90th minute, but it wasn't enough and it was Spurs who went through to the Fourth Round – and ultimately a second successive final, where they lost on penalties to Manchester United.

FA CUP FACTS & FIGURES

FA CUP WINS

11	Manchester United
10	Arsenal
8	Tottenham
7	Aston Villa, Liverpool
6	Blackburn Rovers, Newcastle United

APPEARANCES IN FINAL

18	Manchester United
17	Arsenal
13	Everton, Liverpool, Newcastle United

APPEARANCES IN SEMI-FINAL

26	Arsenal, Manchester United
24	Everton
22	Liverpool
19	Aston Villa, West Brom
18	Blackburn Rovers, Chelsea
17	Newcastle United, Tottenham

FA CUP ODDS AND ENDS

■ **FIRST GAME**
21 January 1893 v Middlesbrough (H), lost 2 – 3

■ **FIRST VICTORY**
27 January 1894 v Sheffield United (H), won 2 - 0

■ **BIGGEST VICTORY**
9 – 0 v Southport (A), 1 February 1932

■ **HEAVIEST DEFEAT**
1 – 7 v Aston Villa (A), 16 February 1895

■ **BIGGEST HOME WIN**
8 – 1 v Notts County, 8 January 1927

■ **HEAVIEST HOME DEFEAT**
0 – 5 v Sheffield United, 10 January 1914

■ **UNBEATEN RUN**
16 games, from January 1951 – January 1953

■ **UNBEATEN AT HOME**
United were unbeaten in the FA Cup at home from 1997 - 2007, 18 games in total.

SEMI-FINAL BEST

Newcastle hold the record for a victory in the FA Cup semi-final with the 6-0 slaughter of Fulham at Anfield in 1908. James Howie and Jock Rutherford got two goals each, and Bill Appleyard and Alex Gardner one a piece.

HIGHEST SCORER

Former Newcastle centre-forward Ian Rush scored more FA Cup goals in the 20th Century than any other player. He got 44 – but only one of them, at Everton in1998, was for United. He scored 39 for Liverpool and four for Chester, including one in Chester's 2-0 third round victory at St. James' Park in 1980! Rush also holds the record for scoring in FA Cup Finals. He scored five times in three appearances with Liverpool.

CAPTAIN JOE HARVEY PROUDLY HOLDS
THE FA CUP ALOFT IN 1951

OLDEST PLAYER

The oldest player ever to play in an FA Cup Final was Newcastle right-back Billy Hampson, who was 39 years and 241 days old when he took the field against Aston Villa at Wembley in 1924.

TWICE TOO OFTEN

Newcastle are the only club to have twice lost two successive FA Cup Finals. United were beaten finalists in 1905 and 1906, and in 1998 and 1999.

FIVES AND THREES

Three Newcastle greats of the past played in five FA Cup Finals. Jimmy Lawrence, Jock Rutherford and Colin Veitch all played in 1905, 1906, 1908, 1910 and 1911. Unfortunately, all three collected a joint-record four losers' medals! Manchester United's Roy Keane has played in six Finals, but the all-time record is held by Arthur Kinnaird, who played in nine for Wanderers and Old Etonians between 1873 and 1883.

MILBURN QUICKEST NO MORE

For 42 years, Wor Jackie Milburn of Newcastle held the record for the fastest Wembley FA Cup Final goal – after 45 seconds against Manchester City in 1955. Roberto di Matteo of Chelsea then stole the record with a 42-second goal against Middlesbrough in 1997. And then in May 2009, Louis Saha netted for Everton against Chelsea after an incredible 26 seconds.

GULLIT FIRST

Ruud Gullit became the first foreign manager to lead a side to victory in the FA Cup Final when he steered Chelsea to a 2-0 victory over Middlesbrough in 1997. Gullit, who also scored against Newcastle in the 1996 FA Cup, managed United to the 1999 Final, when they lost to Manchester United.

SICK MICK

Former United skipper Mick Martin became only the second player ever to be sent off in an FA Cup semi-final when he was dismissed playing for West Bromwich against Ipswich at Highbury in 1978. Only one man – Hull's Arthur Childs in 1930 - had been dismissed in the previous 96 years, but eight have been red-carded since, including Roy Keane, the only player ever to have been sent off twice in FA Cup semi-finals (in 1995 and 1999).

FIRST PENALTY

Newcastle forward Albert Shepherd scored the first-ever FA Cup Final penalty when he fired home his and United's second goal in the 2-0 1910 replay defeat of Barnsley at Goodison Park following a foul on Sandy Higgins.

KENNY'S DUAL ROLE

Ex-Newcastle manager Kenny Dalglish became the first player-manager to win the FA Cup when he led Liverpool to their 1986 triumph.

SUPER STAN

Stan Seymour of Newcastle became the first man to play for and manage the same team in victorious FA Cup Finals. He did so with United in 1924, when he scored in the 2-0 defeat of Aston Villa, and in 1951 and 1952, when United beat Blackpool and Arsenal. Peter McWilliam, who played for Newcastle in the 1910 Final victory over Barnsley, became the first man to play for and manage FA Cup winners when he guided Tottenham to their 1921 Cup win.

BRILLIANT BEASANT

Former Newcastle goalkeeper Dave Beasant became the first goalkeeper to captain FA Cup winners when he saved a John Aldridge penalty for Wimbledon in their 1-0 victory over Liverpool in 1988.

PENALTIES ORDEAL

Penalty shoot-outs were first introduced to settle drawn FA Cup replays in 1991-92, and Newcastle were part of only the tournament's third-ever shoot-out when they lost 4-3 to Bournemouth after a 2-2 draw in the third round at St. James' Park.

SUPER SUPERMAC

Malcolm Macdonald is the only man to score twice in each of two post-war FA Cup Semi-Finals for two different clubs. He did it for Newcastle against Burnley in 1974, and for Arsenal against Orient in 1978.

MAKING LIGHT OF IT

Newcastle staged the first-ever FA Cup-tie between League clubs to be played under floodlights. It was the first round second replay between Darlington and Carlisle in November 1955.

ALL-TIME GREATS

OVER THE LAST THREE ANNUALS, WE'VE PICKED JUST A HANDFUL OF NEWCASTLE UNITED POST-WAR GREATS THAT MAKE UP THE VERY FABRIC OF THE CLUB AND WHO'VE WORN THE SHIRT WITH PRIDE, WHERE MODERN-DAY HEROES SUCH AS LES FERDINAND, PETER BEARDSLEY AND PHILIPPE ALBERT HAVE RUBBED SHOULDERS WITH LEGENDS LIKE GEORGE ROBLEDO, JOE HARVEY AND JIMMY SMITH.

THIS YEAR, HOWEVER, WE THOUGHT WE'D TAKE YOU EVEN FURTHER BACK THROUGH THE HISTORY BOOKS, AND PICK TEN OF OUR ALL-TIME PRE-WAR UNITED GREATS – PLAYERS WHO HELPED LAY THE FOUNDATIONS FOR GENERATIONS TO COME.

ONCE AGAIN, IT'S NOT A DEFINITIVE LIST, AND IN NO PRIORITY OF 'GREATNESS', SO HERE WE GO.

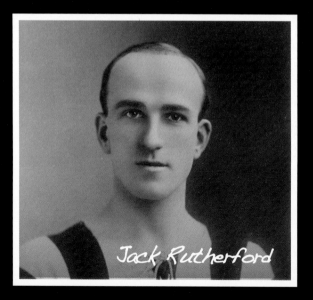

Jack Rutherford

BILL APPLEYARD (1903 -1908)

During the days when goalkeepers were left largely unprotected by referees, heavyweight striker Appleyard was no stranger to some particularly fierce goalmouth skirmishes. It worked to good effect, with the 14 stone former North Sea fisherman, who was given the nickname 'cockles', notching up 88 goals during his five year stint with United, including Newcastle's first ever FA Cup hat-trick against his old club Grimsby.

JACK RUTHERFORD (1902-1913)

Things moved pretty quickly for Geordie boy Jackie Rutherford back at the turn of the 20th century. At the age of just 17, the Percy Main-born forward killed two birds with one stone on his first appearance for United, becoming the Club's youngest ever scorer and, at the time, the youngest debutant. Rutherford went on to become a celebrated forward, earning international recognition with England before he was 20, and scoring 94 goals in 336 appearances for the black and whites.

Andy Aitken

ANDY AITKEN (1895-1906)

Yet another Scot who made his mark in a black and white shirt, Aitken actually took part in United's inaugural First Division game back in 1898 and quickly established himself as an attack-minded midfielder with more than a touch of guile and artistry. Renowned for his versatility, Aitken went on to make 349 appearances for Newcastle, scoring 41 goals along the way and cementing his place among the Club's all-time greats.

HUGHIE GALLACHER (1925-1930)

'Wee Hughie', as he was affectionately known, was perhaps one of the greatest centre-forwards ever to pull on a Newcastle shirt, and at just 5ft 5", what he lacked in height he made up for in goals – and plenty of them. A tenacious striker, Gallacher's United record is as impressive as any, with the Scot lashing an unbelievable 133 goals in just 160 appearances, including 39 in 41 during the 1926/27 season, where he also skippered the side to League title glory.

FRANK HUDSPETH (1910-1929)

Behind the aforementioned Jimmy Lawrence, Frank Hudspeth holds the outfield appearances record for United, with 472 league and cup games under his belt. The Geordie left-back joined the Club from local side North Shields Athletic in 1910 and, alongside Bill McCracken, forged the infamous offside trap that was to become the benchmark of Newcastle's backline. Won the FA Cup with United in 1924 and was an ever-present in the title winning side of 1927.

Colin Veitch

JIMMY LAWRENCE (1904-1922)

Had Shay Given still been a Newcastle player, he may well have been closing in on keeper Jimmy Lawrence's record of 507 appearances for the Magpies by now. As it turns out, his record remains intact, and as impressive today as it was all those years ago. Scotsman Lawrence – a formidable stopper and an integral part of United's great Edwardian side – spent an incredible 14 seasons as United's first-choice goalkeeper, and won three Championship medals during his Tyneside stay.

BILL McCRACKEN (1904-1923)

United have had some colourful full-backs over the years, but without question, one of the most influential was Belfast-born Bill McCracken. Such was his grasp of the offside trap, the often controversial defender forced football's authorities into a tactical rethink and a change of the rules in 1925, and having arrived as a second-choice right-back, the Irish international went on to make the position his own, spending an amazing 19 years as a Newcastle player.

PETER McWILLIAM (1902-1911)

The story goes that Peter McWilliam was on his way to Wearside for trials with rivals Sunderland back in 1902, before United officials stepped in and cheekily hijacked the move and brought the left-half to Gallowgate instead. It turned out to be a shrewd move, with Peter winning the title in his first full season at St. James' Park. A swift and skilful tactician, McWilliam went on to manage Tottenham and Middlesbrough once his playing days were over.

ALBERT SHEPHERD (1908-1914)

Another centre-forward who left his mark on United's history books in spectacular fashion. Shepherd lead the line with lightening pace, and such was his confidence in front of goal, that he once asked United's directors if he could leave a game early provided he scored a hat-trick – which he duly did. Shepherd netted twice during the 1910 FA Cup final win over Barnsley, including the first penalty in a final, and in all, he found the net 92 times in just 123 appearances.

COLIN VEITCH (1899-1915)

Back in the day, there were all-rounders, and then there was Colin Veitch. Barring playing in goal, Veitch appeared in just about every position imaginable during his lengthy stay with United and was lauded as the most versatile player in the country before World War One broke out. Described as "a man who is the master of his job", Heaton-born Veitch was one of the cornerstones of the Club's Edwardian success, scoring 49 goals in 322 appearances.

QUIZ 2.

1 IN WHICH YEAR DID NEWCASTLE UNITED
LAST PLAY AT WEMBLEY?

2 WHO CAPTAINED UNITED TO
THEIR 1969 FAIRS CUP TRIUMPH?

3 WHO DID UNITED PLAY IN THEIR ONLY
LEAGUE CUP FINAL?

4 ALAN SHEARER SCORED HIS 206TH AND
LAST UNITED GOAL AGAINST?

5 WHICH FOUR FORMER UNITED PLAYERS WERE IN THE ENGLAND
TEAM THAT REACHED THE SEMI FINALS OF ITALIA 90?

6 WHICH UNITED LEGEND OPENED THE SCORING
IN THE 1955 FA CUP FINAL?

7 WHICH TEAM DID SHOLA AMEOBI SCORE
HIS FIRST NEWCASTLE HAT-TRICK AGAINST?

8 WHICH TWO OTHER TEAMS DID ALAN SHEARER
PLAY FOR IN ENGLAND?

9 THE SON OF A UNITED GOALKEEPER FROM 1976 PLAYED
FOR THE MAGPIES LAST SEASON. WHO IS HE?

10 WHO WERE UNITED'S CZECH AND TRINIDADIAN
GOALKEEPERS IN THE 1990S?

ANSWERS PAGE 61

PLAYER PROFILES

SHOLA AMEOBI

BORN. **12 OCTOBER 1981, ZARIA, NIGERIA**
DEBUT. **09 SEPTEMBER 2000 V CHELSEA (H)**
PREVIOUS CLUB. **ACADEMY**
APPEARANCES & GOALS. **252/50**

Talented striker with a penchant for the unpredictable. Born in Nigeria, Shola came to England with his parents at the age of five and is a product of the Newcastle United Academy. In 2006/07 he claimed second place, behind Alan Shearer, in the all-time United leading European scorers chart with 12 goals. With over 200 appearances for the Magpies, he reached the 50 goals mark for United last season and should have a key role to play in 2009/10.

JOEY BARTON

BORN. **02 SEPTEMBER 1982, HUYTON, MERSEYSIDE**
DEBUT. **22 OCTOBER 2007 V TOTTENHAM (H)**
PREVIOUS CLUB. **MANCHESTER CITY**
APPEARANCES & GOALS. **32/2**

Joey joined United in June 2007, but a broken metatarsal a month later meant his early season ambitions went up in smoke. The attack-minded combative midfielder, with one England cap to his name, has only made 32 appearances for the Magpies in two seasons, a knee problem holding him back in 2009. However the highly rated Liverpudlian aims to be back in the United engine room where his all-action displays, coupled with goals, will be much needed.

NICKY BUTT

BORN. **21 JANUARY 1975, MANCHESTER**
DEBUT. **14 AUGUST 2004 V MIDDLESBROUGH (A)**
PREVIOUS CLUB. **MANCHESTER UTD, BIRMINGHAM CITY (LOAN)**
APPEARANCES & GOALS. **151/5**

Nicky, a tough tackling but skillful ball-winning midfielder, had a terrific 2008/09 campaign at St. James' Park. Always one of the first names on the team sheet, the 39 times capped England international is United's Mr Consistent. Dedicated, tenacious and with a steely will-to-win, Nicky won nine major titles at Manchester United, and was a Champions League winner in 1999, but is now a firm favourite amongst the Gallowgate faithful.

PLAYER PROFILES

BORN. **06 JANUARY 1989, GATESHEAD**
DEBUT. **02 NOVEMBER 2006 V PALERMO**
PREVIOUS CLUB. **ACADEMY**
APPEARANCES & GOALS. **29/3**

Andy made his first team debut, and became United's youngest ever European debutant in the 1–0 UEFA Cup win in Palermo, Italy, on 02 November 2006. Consistently on target for the second-string in his earlier career, the tall powerful striker, who spent the first half of the 2007/08 season on loan at Preston North End, made his breakthrough at United last season with three goals in five Premier League starts. A key role awaits the likeable Geordie in 2009/10.

FABRICIO COLOCCINI

BORN. **22 JANUARY 1982, CORDOBA**
DEBUT. **17 AUGUST 2008 V MAN UTD (A)**
PREVIOUS CLUB. **AC MILAN, DEPORTIVO LA CORUNA**
APPEARANCES & GOALS. **38/0**

Fabricio joined United from Deportivo La Coruna. He began his career with Argentinos Juniors but made his professional debut in 1998 with Boca Juniors. The following season he moved to AC Milan but spent most of his time at the San Siro out on loan. In 2004, he was an Olympic Gold medallist and he also played in the 2006 World Cup in Germany. In 2007/08, he played every minute of Deportivo's La Liga campaign, and last season played a healthy 34 of United's 38 league games.

RYAN DONALDSON

BORN. **01 MAY 1991, NEWCASTLE**
DEBUT. **N/A**
PREVIOUS CLUB. **ACADEMY**
APPEARANCES & GOALS. **0/0**

 Still a schoolboy at St Cuthberts in Newcastle when he made his reserve team debut in January 2007 at Wigan after impressing for the Academy Under-18 side, ending the campaign with 12 goals in 20 matches. Ryan started off as a striker at United but has since moved back into midfield. He made his England U17 debut in July 2007 and is currently in the Under 19 squad. Yet to appear in the first team, though a regular on the bench, he hopes to make a breakthrough in 2009/10.

PLAYER PROFILES

JOSE ENRIQUE

BORN. 23 JANUARY 1986, VALENCIA, SPAIN
DEBUT. 29 AUGUST 2007 V BARNSLEY (H)
PREVIOUS CLUB. LEVANTE, VILLARREAL
APPEARANCES & GOALS. 56/0

Popular Spaniard Jose Enrique joined the Magpies from Villarreal in August 2007 and, after a slow start to his United career, settled in to the left-back slot with some adventurous attacking displays complimenting his committed defensive displays. The Spain U21 international was nicknamed 'The Bull' in his homeland – his fierce tackling earning him that tag. Jose began his career at Levante and also had a season on loan at Celta Vigo.

FRASER FORSTER

BORN. 17 MARCH 1988, HEXHAM
DEBUT. N/A
PREVIOUS CLUB. ACADEMY
APPEARANCES & GOALS. 0/0

Fraser joined the Newcastle United Academy in 2005 from the Royal Grammar School in Newcastle and last season, along with Tim Krul, was deputy to Steve Harper after Shay Given had moved on to Manchester City. Tall and agile, Fraser has turned in some outstanding performances for the Reserves whilst waiting to make his first-team bow. He gained some valuable Football League experience at Stockport in October 2008.

GEREMI

BORN. 20 DECEMBER 1978, BAFOUSSAM, CAMEROON
DEBUT. 11 AUGUST 2007 V BOLTON (A)
PREVIOUS CLUB. REAL MADRID, MIDDLESBROUGH, CHELSEA
APPEARANCES & GOALS. 45/1

Affable, seasoned international midfielder who has enjoyed two seasons on Tyneside. Shares the honour amongst the squad, alongside Nicky Butt, of being a Champions League winner. Geremi represented Cameroon in the Africa Cup of Nations in Ghana in 2008, reaching the Final before losing to Egypt. He later won his 100th International cap against Guinea on 11 February 2009. Holder of an Olympic Gold medal from the Sydney games in 2000.

PLAYER PROFILES

DANNY GUTHRIE

BORN. **18 APRIL 1987, SHREWSBURY**
DEBUT. **17 AUGUST 2008 V MAN UTD (A)**
PREVIOUS CLUB. **LIVERPOOL, BOLTON, SOUTHAMPTON**
APPEARANCES & GOALS. **27/2**

Danny signed for United in July 2008 from Liverpool, having spent the 2007/08 season on loan at Bolton Wanderers where he played 35 games, seven of which were in the UEFA Cup. He only made three Premier League appearances for Liverpool but, last season, proved what an astute acquisition he had been with a number of solid and consistent displays in the United engine room. A strong-running competitive midfielder, a fruitful 2009/10 campaign hopefully awaits.

JONAS GUTIERREZ

BORN. **05 JULY 1983, BUENOS AIRES, ARGENTINA**
DEBUT. **17 AUGUST 2008 V MAN UTD (A)**
PREVIOUS CLUB. **RCD MALLORCA, VELEZ SARSFIELD**
APPEARANCES & GOALS. **33/0**

Argentina international Jonas Gutierrez was Newcastle United's first signing in the 2008 close season. The right-sided attacker has the nickname 'Spiderman' for wearing the superhero's webbed mask during flamboyant goal celebrations. Jonas began his career with Velez Sarsfield in his native Argentina in 2001, helping the club win the Primera Division title in 2005 before moving to Mallorca in Spain. His endeavour and enterprise brought him many admirers last season.

STEVE HARPER

BORN. **14 MARCH 1975, EASINGTON**
DEBUT. **BRADFORD CITY, HARTLEPOOL, HUDDERSFIELD (LOANS)**
PREVIOUS CLUB. **28 NOVEMBER 1998 V WIMBLEDON (H)**
APPEARANCES & GOALS. **127/0**

United's No 1 after the sale of Shay Given to Manchester City. Very popular on and off the pitch at St. James' Park, the Easington-born shot-stopper is one of the top English goalkeepers in the country. He first broke into the first team during the 1998/99 season and then played in the 1999 FA Cup Final against Manchester United in only his 10th senior match. Possesses terrific reflexes and is a commanding presence in the 18-yard box.

PLAYER PROFILES

TAMAS KADAR

BORN. **14 MARCH 1990, VESZPREM, HUNGARY**
DEBUT. -
PREVIOUS CLUB. **ZALAEGERSZEGI**
APPEARANCES & GOALS. **0/0**

Defender Tamas joined United from Hungarian outfit Zalaegerszegi TE for whom he made his debut when only 16. He played 14 times for Zala', scoring once. Clever on the ball with a good eye for a pass, Tamas has a great engine too, making him a real 90-minute player. Made the United first team bench for the first time against Liverpool at SJP on 28 December 2008 but a broken leg a few weeks later halted his progress. Played in the 2009/10 pre-season friendly games.

TIM KRUL

BORN. **03 APRIL 1988, DEN HAAG, HOLLAND**
DEBUT. **02 NOVEMBER 2006 V PALMERO (A)**
PREVIOUS CLUB. **DEN HAAG**
APPEARANCES & GOALS. **1/0**

Tim joined United from Dutch side Den Haag in July 2005. The Dutch youth international goalkeeper made his debut in the UEFA Cup against Palmero in Sicily in November 2006, turning in a man of the match performance. Although yet to make a Football League appearance for United before the start of the 2009/10 campaign, he did spend part of 2007/08 on loan at SPL side Falkirk where he made 26 appearances – Tim has terrific potential and time is on his side.

KAZENGA LUALUA

BORN. **10 DECEMBER 1990, KINSHASA, CONGO**
DEBUT. **06 JANUARY 2008 V STOKE (A)**
PREVIOUS CLUB. **ACADEMY**
APPEARANCES & GOALS. **9/0**

Hugely talented young striker with a high level of skill and great range of trickery. A product of the Newcastle United Academy, Kazenga is the younger brother of Lomana who made 88 appearances for United. Kazenga has impressed in the limited time he has been on the field in first-team matches since making his bow in the FA Cup at Stoke in January 2008. Unpredictable and the scorer of some outstanding goals, he aims to make his mark during 2009/10.

PLAYER PROFILES

KEVIN NOLAN

BORN. **24 JUNE 1982, LIVERPOOL**
DEBUT. **01 FEBRUARY 2009 V SUNDERLAND (H)**
PREVIOUS CLUB. **BOLTON**
APPEARANCES & GOALS. **11/0**

Kevin Nolan joined United in January 2009, moving from Bolton having spent his entire senior career at the Reebok. Liverpool born, he played for the City's schoolboys at 14 but joined Wanderers at 15 and two years later signed professional terms for the Trotters. He made his United debut against local rivals Sunderland and immediately got caught up in the passion that surrounds North East football. A strong, popular figure, his battling qualities will serve United well.

NILE RANGER

BORN. **11 APRIL 1991, LONDON**
DEBUT. **N/A**
PREVIOUS CLUB. **ACADEMY**
APPEARANCES & GOALS. **0/0**

The London born striker was originally with Southampton but joined the United set up in July 2008. He scored on his Academy debut at Leicester and sat on the first team bench at Coventry in a League Cup tie three days later without getting on. Nile won the 'Wor Jackie' award from Sport Newcastle in March 2009 and in four England Under-19 games in the summer of 2009, scored four goals. He hit 22 goals in 43 Reserve and Youth games in 2008/09.

ALAN SMITH

BORN. **28 OCTOBER 1980, ROTHWELL, LEEDS**
DEBUT. **11 AUGUST 2007 V BOLTON**
PREVIOUS CLUB. **LEEDS UTD, MANCHESTER UTD**
APPEARANCES & GOALS. **43/0**

A gritty and determined front man, Smith possesses great strength and is adaptable enough to fill a midfield role too with great aplomb. He scored on his Premiership debut for Leeds, when only 18, before moving to Manchester United where incredibly he also scored on his debut. The sort of player you want on your side in a battle, which the Championship may well be, Smith could play a key role in United's quest for promotion.

PLAYER PROFILES

RYAN TAYLOR

BORN. **19 AUGUST 1984, LIVERPOOL**
DEBUT. **07 FEBRUARY 2009 V WEST BROM (A)**
PREVIOUS CLUB. **TRANMERE, WIGAN**
APPEARANCES & GOALS. **10/0**

Ryan Taylor signed for United in February 2009 from Wigan as part of the deal that saw Charles N'Zogbia move in the opposite direction. Ryan began his career at Tranmere before a £750,000 move to the JJB in 2005. Able to fill both the full-back berths, Ryan is a hard tackling defender, comfortable on the ball and with bundles of energy. Possesses a deadly free-kick and also a long throw which makes him a very dangerous opponent. His versatility should serve United well.

STEVEN TAYLOR

BORN. **23 JANUARY 1986, GREENWICH, LONDON**
DEBUT. **25 MARCH 2004 V REAL MALLORCA (A)**
PREVIOUS CLUB. **WYCOMBE (LOAN)**
APPEARANCES & GOALS. **150/9**

Steven, a powerful and dominating centre-half, was a solid performer in United's back four during 2008/09 in a season when the defence was often 'under the cosh'. A leader in the best Geordie traditions, his passion and will-to-win for himself, the team, and the supporters is unbridled. Formerly captain of the England Under-21 team, he has also represented England 'B'. Off the field, Steven is the perfect ambassador for United.

XISCO

BORN. **26 JUNE 1986, MALLORCA**
DEBUT. **13 SEPTEMBER 2008 V HULL CITY (H)**
PREVIOUS CLUB. **DEPORTIVO LA CORUNA**
APPEARANCES & GOALS. **7/1**

Francisco Jimenez Tejada, aka Xisco, joined the Magpies in September 2008. The Mallorca born Spain U21 striker is recognized as the most successful player to come out of Deportivo since the Galicians returned to the Primera Division in 1991, his goals helping Depor into the 2008/09 UEFA Cup. Xisco only made a limited impact at United last season but hopes 2009/10 will bring greater reward. He did score on his United debut against Hull City.

FA CUP SNAKES & LADDERS

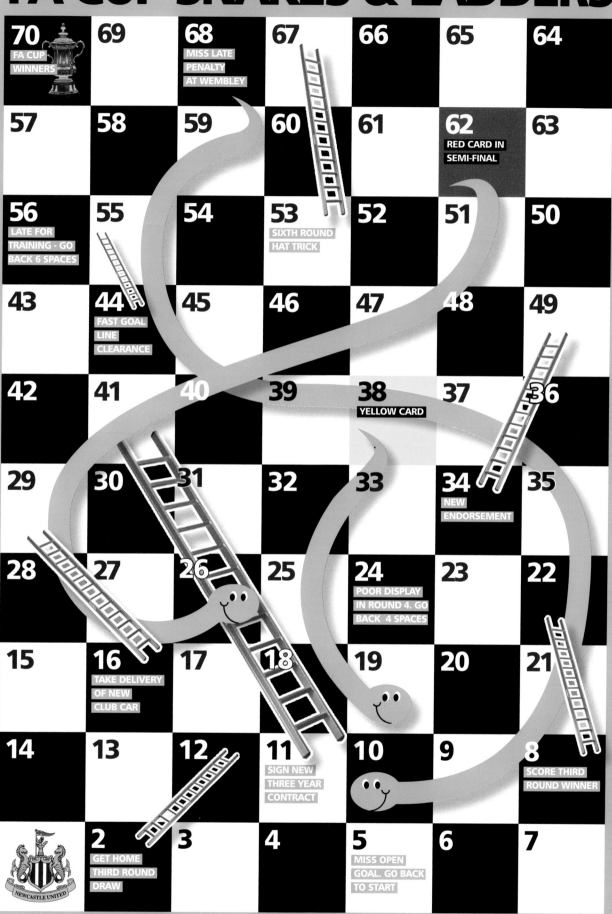

SIR
BOBBY ROBSON

A LIFE IN FOOTBALL 1933-2009

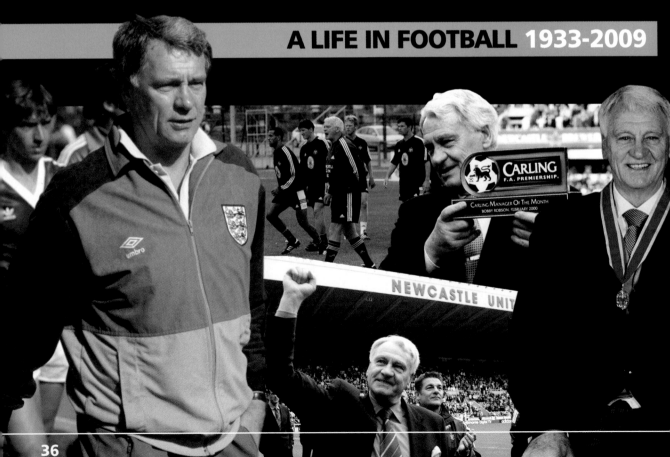

WORD SEARCH

SEE IF YOU CAN FIND 20 PLAYERS FROM THE LAST 15 YEARS OF THE PREMIER LEAGUE – 10 NEWCASTLE UNITED AND 10 FROM OTHER CLUBS HIDDEN IN THE WORD SEARCH BELOW.

Y	Q	L	H	A	N	O	T	N	A	C	H	T	J	E	T	T
U	W	K	G	I	N	O	L	A	U	F	Q	H	E	N	R	Y
J	E	J	J	Q	D	P	M	D	I	D	Y	U	N	F	E	G
N	B	H	K	W	N	K	P	A	R	O	L	Y	A	T	W	B
V	E	G	L	E	A	N	Q	M	D	S	K	K	S	O	P	T
J	A	M	E	S	N	G	R	S	E	A	T	D	P	R	L	C
G	F	R	Z	R	I	D	H	C	T	Q	V	T	Q	R	R	E
J	D	D	X	T	D	A	L	F	H	W	S	G	R	E	N	T
W	S	S	B	E	R	G	K	A	M	P	Z	O	B	S	R	A
E	L	A	C	Y	E	A	O	N	J	E	O	H	S	E	N	G
B	E	R	E	S	F	O	R	D	L	N	L	J	P	D	C	D
O	Y	Q	V	U	A	Q	I	N	E	R	A	R	E	W	W	O
O	V	W	B	B	O	W	U	Y	L	T	A	K	E	P	R	O
P	B	E	G	I	B	E	T	P	W	H	P	K	D	A	H	W
L	N	O	N	O	N	R	F	Q	E	Y	P	L	S	G	L	U
J	R	T	M	P	M	T	Z	R	R	T	E	N	A	E	K	K

BEARDSLEY	ADAMS
BERESFORD	BERGKAMP
FERDINAND	CANTONA
GINOLA	DROGBA
HARPER	HENRY
JENAS	JAMES
SOLANO	KEANE
SPEED	ROONEY
TAYLOR	TORRES
WOODGATE	ZOLA

ANSWERS PAGE 61

ALL-TIME OPPOSITION

NEWCASTLE UNITED HAVE PLAYED 164 OTHER TEAMS COMPETITIVELY IN THEIR ILLUSTRIOUS HISTORY, FROM THE WELSH MINNOWS OF ABERDARE WHOM UNITED BEAT IN THE FA CUP IN 1926 TO CURRENT EUROPEAN CHAMPIONS BARCELONA.

	Pl	W	D	L	F	A
A						
ABERDARE	1	1	0	0	4	1
ANDERLECHT	2	1	0	1	3	3
ATHLETIC BILBAO	2	1	0	1	3	3
ARSENAL	165	65	36	64	229	234
ASTON VILLA	149	64	31	54	233	237
AZ ALKMAAR	2	1	0	1	4	4
B						
BARCELONA	4	1	0	3	4	8
BARNSLEY	39	17	11	11	60	40
BASEL	2	2	0	0	4	2
BASTIA	2	0	0	2	2	5
BAYER LEVERKUSEN	2	2	0	0	6	2
BEDFORD TOWN	1	0	0	1	1	2
BIRMINGHAM CITY	100	39	28	33	156	140
BLACKBURN ROVERS	135	55	29	51	203	200
BLACKPOOL	57	25	8	24	91	99
BOHEMIANS	2	1	1	0	4	0
BOLTON WANDERERS	114	53	20	41	200	147
BOURNEMOUTH	6	2	2	2	9	6
BRADFORD CITY	42	20	9	13	68	50
BRADFORD PARK AVE	21	12	3	6	38	18
NAC BREDA	2	2	0	0	6	0
BRENTFORD	9	6	0	3	19	4
BRIGHTON	16	7	3	6	27	17
BRISTOL CITY	24	10	8	6	40	21
BRISTOL ROVERS	19	8	7	4	27	18

	Pl	W	D	L	F	A
B (CONT)						
BURTON SWIFTS	10	5	0	5	26	23
BURY	68	36	14	18	143	95
C						
CAMBRIDGE UNITED	16	9	3	4	21	9
CARDIFF CITY	49	21	13	15	84	59
CARLISLE UNITED	7	3	1	3	11	10
CELTA VIGO	1	1	0	0	2	1
CHARLTON ATHLETIC	70	30	20	20	115	96
CHELSEA	145	47	37	61	179	214
CHELTENHAM	1	1	0	0	2	0
CHESTER	4	1	1	2	3	4
CHESTERFIELD	11	4	0	7	13	17
COLCHESTER UNITED	3	1	1	1	6	8
CORINTHIANS	1	1	0	0	3	1
COVENTRY CITY	66	32	16	18	127	80
CREWE ALEXANDRA	8	5	1	2	21	10
CROATIA ZAGREB	2	1	1	0	4	3
CRYSTAL PALACE	30	18	4	8	44	23
CSKA SOFIA	2	1	1	0	4	2
D						
DARWEN	8	5	1	2	24	17
DEPORTIVO LA CORUNA	2	0	0	2	2	4
DERBY COUNTY	119	50	32	37	183	152
DINAMO TBLISI	1	1	0	0	2	0
DONCASTER ROVERS	7	6	1	0	24	6
DUNDEE UNITED	2	2	0	0	3	1

	Pl	W	D	L	F	A
D (CONT)						
DYNAMO KIEV	4	2	1	1	6	5
E						
EINTRACHT FRANKFURT	1	0	1	0	0	0
EVERTON	156	62	34	60	234	228
EXETER CITY	2	0	1	1	1	5
F						
FENERBAHCE	1	1	0	0	1	0
FERENCVAROS	2	1	0	1	6	3
FEYENOORD	4	2	0	2	7	5
FULHAM	61	24	12	25	113	98
G						
GAINSBOROUGH TOWN	4	2	0	2	9	7
GILLINGHAM	1	1	0	0	2	1
GLOSSOP	3	2	1	0	2	0
GRIMSBY TOWN	41	16	9	16	66	51
H						
HALIFAX TOWN	1	1	0	0	2	1
HALMSTADS	2	1	0	1	5	2
HAPOEL BENI SAKHNIN	2	2	0	0	4	2
HARTLEPOOL UNITED	1	1	0	0	2	1
HENDON	2	1	1	0	5	1
HEERENVEEN	2	2	0	0	4	2
HEREFORD UNITED	2	0	1	1	3	4
HUDDERSFIELD TOWN	59	24	15	20	94	81
HULL CITY	20	10	5	5	38	20
I						
INTER MILAN	4	1	2	1	6	7
IPSWICH TOWN	45	15	14	16	68	56
J						
JUVENTUS	2	1	0	1	1	2
L						
LEEDS UNITED	91	37	17	37	127	144
LEICESTER CITY	112	48	26	38	184	177
LEVADIA TALLINN	2	2	0	0	3	1
LEYTON ORIENT	21	9	5	7	34	20
LILLESTROM	2	1	1	0	4	1
LINCOLN CITY	11	7	0	4	27	18
LIVERPOOL	159	45	38	76	194	275
LOUGHBOROUGH TOWN	6	4	0	2	11	6
LUTON TOWN	50	22	11	17	89	78
M						
MANCHESTER CITY	161	70	38	53	244	219
MANCHESTER UNITED	148	39	35	74	218	286
MANSFIELD TOWN	3	2	1	0	3	1
MARSEILLE	2	0	1	1	0	2
METZ	2	1	1	0	8	3
MIDDLESBROUGH	123	48	36	39	178	152
MIDDLESBROUGH IRON	2	1	1	0	8	3
MILLWALL	18	5	4	9	19	26
MONACO	2	0	0	2	0	4

	Pl	W	D	L	F	A
M (CONT)						
MUNICH 1860	2	2	0	0	6	3
N						
NEWPORT COUNTY	3	2	0	1	21	4
NORTHAMPTON TOWN	9	4	2	3	16	11
NORTHWICH VICTORIA	2	1	0	1	6	5
NORWICH CITY	46	19	13	14	73	53
NOTTINGHAM FOREST	104	48	27	29	162	121
NOTTS COUNTY	64	32	15	17	134	74
O						
OLDHAM ATHLETIC	40	18	12	10	63	42
OLYMPIACOS	2	2	0	0	7	1
OXFORD UNITED	17	6	5	6	30	30
P						
PALERMO	1	1	0	0	1	0
PANIONIOS	1	1	0	0	1	0
PARTIZAN BELGRADE	4	2	0	2	3	3
PECSI DOZSA	2	1	0	1	2	2
PETERBOROUGH UNITED	8	4	1	3	14	9
PLYMOUTH ARGYLE	33	19	8	6	64	34
PORTO	2	1	1	0	1	0
PORT VALE	18	9	5	4	35	26
PORTSMOUTH	69	30	18	21	102	99
PRESTON NE	77	33	12	32	121	124
PSV EINDHOVEN	4	1	1	2	3	5
Q						
QUEENS PARK RANGERS	40	18	6	16	60	65
R						
RANGERS	2	1	1	0	2	0
READING	10	6	1	3	25	13
REAL MALLORCA	2	2	0	0	7	1
REAL ZARAGOZA	2	1	0	1	4	4
RENDAL	1	1	0	0	5	0
ROMA	2	0	1	1	0	1
ROTHERHAM UNITED	21	11	6	4	49	23
ROYAL ANTWERP	2	2	0	0	10	2
S						
SCUNTHORPE UNITED	10	4	2	4	12	9
SHEFFIELD UNITED	121	43	29	49	176	175
SHEFFIELD WEDNESDAY	125	56	30	39	201	161
SHREWSBURY TOWN	10	4	2	4	12	9
SOCHAUX	1	1	0	0	4	0
SOUTHAMPTON	84	34	19	31	126	112
SOUTHEND UNITED	4	2	1	1	7	9
SOUTHPORT	5	3	2	0	19	2
SPORTING LISBON	5	2	2	1	5	6
SPORTING LOKEREN	2	2	0	0	5	0
STOCKPORT COUNTY	3	2	1	0	7	1
STOCKTON	1	1	4	0	1	1
STOKE CITY	79	39	19	21	138	89
SUNDERLAND	141	51	46	44	212	222

	Pl	W	D	L	F	A
S (CONT)						
SWANSEA CITY	32	20	3	9	64	38
SWINDON TOWN	17	7	6	4	36	17
T						
TORQUAY UNITED	1	1	0	0	3	1
TOTTENHAM HOTSPUR	142	53	30	59	212	222
TOW LAW TOWN	1	1	0	0	4	0
TRANMERE ROVERS	9	7	0	2	21	9
TROYES	2	0	2	0	4	4
U						
UJPEST DOZSA	2	2	0	0	6	2
V						
VALERENGA IF	2	1	1	0	4	2
FK VENTSPILS	2	1	1	0	1	0
VITORIA SETUBAL	2	1	0	1	6	4
W						
WALSALL	14	11	0	3	32	12

	Pl	W	D	L	F	A
W (CONT)						
WATFORD	34	12	14	8	46	38
WEST BROMWICH A	111	41	28	42	185	184
WEST HAM UNITED	119	47	35	37	182	168
WEST HARTLEPOOL NER	1	1	0	0	8	0
WILLINGTON A	1	1	0	0	6	0
WIMBLEDON	23	7	6	10	38	40
WIGAN ATHLETIC	11	4	2	5	13	13
WOLVERHAMPTON W	87	28	21	38	137	144
WREXHAM	10	3	3	4	12	14
Y						
YEADING	1	1	0	0	2	0
YORK CITY	4	2	2	0	6	3
Z						
ZELJEZNICAR	2	2	0	0	5	0
ZULTE WAREGEM	2	2	0	0	4	1
FC ZURICH	2	2	0	0	5	2

164 different teams. (Middlesbrough 1, AZ Alkmaar 164). Current League teams Newcastle have never played (11): Accrington, Aldershot, Barnet, Burton, Dagenham, Darlington, Macclesfield, Morecambe, Rochdale, Wycombe, Yeovil

TOTAL RECORD (1892/93 - 2008/9)

Away record includes neutral ground for FA Cup/League Cup/Charity Shield. All competitive games 1892/93 to 2008/9 inclusive.

	HOME						AWAY						TOTAL					
	Pl	W	D	L	F	A	Pl	W	D	L	F	A	Pl	W	D	L	F	A
PREMIER LEAGUE	308	169	75	64	539	314	308	78	90	140	345	463	616	247	165	204	884	777
DIVISION 1	1272	689	284	299	2463	1512	1272	302	322	648	1492	2262	2544	991	606	947	3955	3774
DIVISION 2	523	337	100	86	1154	527	523	144	118	261	644	911	1046	481	218	347	1798	1438
FL TEST/PLAYOFFS	3	2	0	1	6	3	3	0	1	2	3	5	6	2	1	3	9	8
NORTHERN LEAGUE	5	3	1	1	16	6	5	2	0	3	15	14	10	5	1	4	31	20
FA CUP	173	101	40	32	371	180	185	74	44	67	276	254	358	175	84	99	647	434
LEAGUE CUP	56	33	8	15	106	56	65	19	11	35	81	104	121	52	19	50	187	160
CHARITY SHIELD	1	0	0	1	3	5	6	2	0	4	10	15	7	2	0	5	13	20
EUROPE	60	44	8	8	123	47	60	25	14	21	85	72	120	69	22	29	108	119
WAR TIME (LGE CUP)	138	85	19	34	41	229	129	42	18	69	249	290	267	127	37	103	654	510
ANGLO ITALIAN	6	4	1	1	17	5	7	3	3	1	9	7	13	7	4	2	26	12
TEXACO CUP	14	10	3	1	36	14	14	2	5	7	13	17	28	12	8	8	49	31
ANGLO SCOT CUP	3	1	1	1	5	4	4	1	1	2	1	5	7	2	2	3	6	9
CORONATION CUP	0	0	0	0	0	0	0	1	0	0	2	5	1	0	0	1	2	5
SIMOD CUP	1	1	0	0	2	1	1	0	0	2	2	4	3	1	0	2	4	5
FULL MEMBERS CUP	0	0	0	0	0	0	1	0	0	1	2	5	1	0	0	1	2	5
MERCANTILE TROPHY	1	1	0	0	1	0	1	0	0	1	1	2	2	1	0	1	2	2
ZENITH DATA CUP	2	2	0	0	5	2	3	0	1	2	7	9	5	2	1	2	12	11
ANULLED MATCHES	2	2	0	0	12	4	2	0	0	2	0	5	4	2	0	2	12	9
TOTAL	2568	1484	540	544	5273	2900	2592	695	628	1269	3229	4448	5160	2179	1168	1813	8502	7348

WHERE ARE THEY NOW?

IT'S ALWAYS INTERESTING TO FIND OUT WHAT FORMER PLAYERS WHO HAVE GRACED THE ST. JAMES' PARK TURF IN RECENT YEARS ARE DOING WITH THEIR LIVES. HERE'S A SELECTION FROM THE PAST 15 YEARS.

PHILIPPE ALBERT

CENTRE HALF 1994–99
138 APPS, 12 GOALS

After leaving Newcastle In 1999, Albert chose to return to Belgium to play for Charleroi before retiring in 2000. He is now working as a pundit for Belgian TV, whilst at the same time running a successful fruit and vegetable business in Belgium.

WARREN BARTON

RIGHT BACK 1995-2002
220 APPS, 5 GOALS

Part of Kevin Keegan's 'Entertainers', Warren works for Fox Soccer Channel in the USA as a pundit. He was also the U18s coach at LA Galaxy for a short spell. After leaving United, he also ran a sports travel business as well as working for Sky as an analyst.

DAVID BATTY

MIDFIELD 1996-1998
114 APPS, 4 GOALS

Since his retirement, David has featured in Sky One's 'The Match' as well as being involved in advertising campaigns for cancer research alongside Alan Hansen, John Hartson and Les Ferdinand to raise the awareness of prostate cancer.

JOHN BERESFORD

LEFT BACK 1992 – 1998
232 APPS, 8 GOALS

After retiring at Birmingham City after his loan spell in 1994, John went on to represent the England Beach Soccer Team. He is currently a pundit for ITV Tyne Tees and ESPN as well as working as a matchday host at St. James' Park.

PETER BEARDSLEY

STRIKER 1983-1987 & 1993-1997
326 APPS, 119 GOALS

The United legend had a fabulous playing career, which also included two World Cups. The scorer of many memorable goals is now coaching in the United Academy, passing on his experience and knowledge to United's up and coming youngsters.

LEE CLARK

MIDFIELD 1988–1997 & 2004-05
265 APPS, 28 GOALS

Brought into the side by Ossie Ardiles he enjoyed two fruitful spells on Tyneside. Since retiring, Lee took charge of the reserves at St. James' Park before moving on to take the job of manager at Huddersfield Town in 2008. A real Geordie character.

NIKOS DABIZAS

CENTRE HALF 1998 – 2004
138 APPS, 12 GOALS

Whole-hearted defender, after leaving Leicester City in 2005 he penned a three-year contract with Greek team Larissa, and in 2007 led his side to the Greek Cup. Remembered by many for his winner at the Stadium of Light in 2002.

DAVID GINOLA

WINGER 1995 – 1997
75 APPS, 7 GOALS

Since his retirement from football, Ginola has acted in two films, 'Mr. Firecul' and 'The Last Drop'and also continues to endorse L'Oreal hair products. In 2008, Ginola received a silver medal at the International Wine Challenge for a rosé wine produced at his vineyard in Provence.

LES FERDINAND

CENTRE FORWARD 1995 – 1997
83 APPS, 50 GOALS

'Sir Les', now the forwards coach at Tottenham Hotspur, was a pundit for BBC and Setanta in 2007/08. He has founded Team48 Motorsport with former footballers John Barnes and Luther Blisset, which aims to promote young Afro-Caribbean racing drivers.

ROB LEE

MIDFIELD 1992 – 2002
381 APPS, 56 GOALS

A Newcastle stalwart, after ending his playing career in 2006 with League 2 side Wycombe, he currently works as a regular pundit for Singapore's Football channel. He is also a regular contributor to Sky Sports and works alongside former United goalkeeper John Burridge for Ten Sports UEFA Champions League fixtures.

TEMURI KETSBAIA

FORWARD 1997 – 2000
108 APPS, 14 GOALS

Since ending his playing days in 2006, Temuri went on to manage Anorthosis Famagusta in Cyprus before moving on to Greek side Olympiacos. Fondly remembered on Tyneside for his Champions League goal against Croatia Zagreb and for kicking the advertising hoarding after scoring against Bolton in 1998.

CHRIS WADDLE

WINGER 1980 – 1985
191 APPS, 52 GOALS

A member of United's promotion winning team in 1984, Chris now frequently appears on BBC Radio Five Live as a summariser and was also a regular with Setanta whilst they covered Premier League matches in 2008/09. He also writes a column in 'The Sun' newspaper.

PAVEL SRNICEK

GOALKEEPER 1990 – 98 & 2006
138 APPS, 12 GOALS

Since his release from Newcastle at the end of the 2006/07 season, Pavel, a cult hero on Tyneside, has begun the Srnicek school of goalkeeping in the Czech Republic, offering youngsters from around the world the chance to learn from his unique coaching style. He is also involved in a number of charity organisations.

NOLBERTO SOLANO

MIDFIELD/WINGER 1998 – 2004
315 APPS, 48 GOALS

After leaving the Premier League at the end of the 2007/08 season, Nobby joined up with Nikos Dabizas and Laurent Robert at Larissa. He is now back home in Peru, where he is a national hero, and playing for Universitario de Deportes. Famed for his trumpet playing whilst with the Magpies.

LAURENT ROBERT

LEFT WING 2001 – 2005
181 APPS, 32 GOALS

The enigmatic Frenchman, who played his best football under Sir Bobby Robson, has joined up with ex Newcastle United team mate Nikos Dabizas at Super League Greece side Larissa FC.

DID YOU KNOW...?

1893-94

THE HOME WIN OVER MIDDLESBROUGH IRONOPOLIS WAS THE FIRST OCCURRENCE OF A 7-2 SCORELINE IN THE HISTORY OF THE FOOTBALL LEAGUE.

1897-98

UNITED LOST ONLY SIX TIMES IN THE LEAGUE, AND CONCEDED ONLY 32 GOALS, BOTH CLUB RECORDS.

1904-05

UNITED PLAYED IN FRONT OF 101,117 IN THE FA CUP FINAL, THE BIGGEST CROWD THAT HAS EVER WATCHED THEM PLAY.

1907-08

THE 6-0 WIN OVER FULHAM IS A RECORD VICTORY IN ANY FA CUP SEMI-FINAL.

1910-11

THE FA CUP FINAL AGAINST BRADFORD CITY (1-1) WAS THE LAST TO BE PLAYED WITHOUT EXTRA-TIME IN THE EVENT OF A DRAW.

1911-12

IN THE AWAY GAME AT MANCHESTER CITY, THE HOME SIDE MISSED THREE PENALTIES, THE ONLY TIME THIS HAS HAPPENED IN THE TOP DIVISION.

1923-24

THE FA CUP FINAL AGAINST ASTON VILLA AT WEMBLEY WAS THE FIRST SHOWPIECE GAME TO BE AN ALL-TICKET MATCH.

1926-27

THE FIXTURE AGAINST CORINTHIANS WAS THE FIRST FA CUP TIE FOR WHICH A RUNNING COMMENTARY WAS BROADCAST ON RADIO.

1929-30

ANDY CUNNINGHAM BECAME THE FIRST EVER PLAYER-MANAGER IN DIVISION ONE.

1930-31

UNITED'S RECORD ST. JAMES' PARK ATTENDANCE OF 68,386 WAS SET AGAINST CHELSEA.

1931-32

THE FA CUP FINAL AGAINST ARSENAL WAS THE LAST IN WHICH PLAYERS WORE UNNUMBERED SHIRTS, AND UNITED BECAME THE FIRST SIDE TO COME FROM BEHIND IN THE FINAL TO WIN THE CUP.

1933-34

UNITED WERE RELEGATED DESPITE BEATING EVERTON 7-3 AWAY AND LIVERPOOL 9-2 AT HOME!

1936-37

THE LONDON & NORTH EAST RAILWAY INTRODUCED A NUMBER OF LOCOMOTIVES BEARING THE NAMES OF FOOTBALL LEAGUE CLUBS, ONE OF WHICH WAS 'NEWCASTLE UNITED'.

1946-47

THE 13-0 WIN OVER NEWPORT COUNTY IS THE CLUB'S RECORD LEAGUE WIN, AND A RECORD MARGIN OF VICTORY FOR ANY MATCH IN THE TOP TWO DIVISIONS.

1951-52

THE FA CUP FINAL WAS THE FIRST FINAL TO FEATURE TWO FOREIGN PLAYERS, UNITED'S ROBLEDO BROTHERS.

1955-56

THE AWAY GAME AT PORTSMOUTH WAS THE FIRST EVER FOOTBALL LEAGUE FLOODLIT GAME.

1959-60

AMAZINGLY, UNITED LOST THEIR OPENING HOME GAME OF THE CAMPAIGN 5-1 FOR THE SECOND SUCCESSIVE SEASON.

1961-62

UNITED WON THE FA YOUTH CUP FOR THE FIRST TIME, BEATING WOLVES IN THE FINAL.

1962/63

UNITED'S FA CUP TIE WITH BRADFORD WAS POSTPONED AN INCREDIBLE 12 TIMES DUE TO BAD WEATHER.

1964-65

THE MAGPIES APPEARED ON BBC MATCH OF THE DAY FOR THE FIRST TIME, AT LEYTON ORIENT.

1965/66

OLLIE BURTON, LATER TO BE A FAIRS CUP WINNER IN 1969, WAS UNITED'S FIRST SUBSTITUTE TO PLAY IN THE LEAGUE. TWO YEARS LATER HE BECAME THE FIRST SUBSTITUTE TO SCORE FOR UNITED!

1971-72

JOHN MOTSON MADE HIS MATCH OF THE DAY DEBUT COMMENTATING ON UNITED'S FA CUP LOSS AT HEREFORD.

1972-73

UNITED BEAT LEEDS 3-2 AT ST. JAMES' PARK, AMAZINGLY IT WAS 2-2 AFTER ONLY EIGHT MINUTES.

1974-75

MALCOLM MACDONALD WAS THE LEAGUE'S TOP SCORER (21), HE ALSO NETTED FIVE TIMES FOR ENGLAND AGAINST CYPRUS.

1979-80

ALAN SHOULDER SCORED NINE PENALTIES DURING THE SEASON – A CLUB RECORD.

1980-81

BALL-BOYS WERE USED FOR THE FIRST TIME AT ST. JAMES' PARK.

1984-85

THE HOME FIXTURE WITH LIVERPOOL WAS UNITED'S FIRST EVER HOME SUNDAY MATCH, AND THE FIRST LEAGUE MATCH TO BE TELEVISED LIVE.

1985-86

IN THE 8-1 AWAY DEFEAT AT WEST HAM, UNITED USED THREE GOALKEEPERS, MARTIN THOMAS, PLUS OUTFIELD PLAYERS CHRIS HEDWORTH AND PETER BEARDSLEY.

1990-91

IN THE AWAY GAME AT WOLVES, STEVE WATSON BECAME THE CLUB'S YOUNGEST DEBUTANT, 16 YEARS AND 223 DAYS.

1991-92

UNITED FIELDED THE YOUNGEST SIDE IN THEIR HISTORY AGAINST BLACKBURN, 21 YEARS AND 303 DAYS.

1992-93

UNITED BEGAN THE SEASON WITH A CLUB RECORD 11 VICTORIES. THE PICTURE ON THE OPPOSITE PAGE SHOWS LIAM O'BRIEN'S WINNER AT ROKER PARK.

1993-94

ANDY COLE SET A NEW CLUB RECORD OF 41 LEAGUE AND CUP GOALS.

1997-98

UNITED PLAYED IN THE UEFA CHAMPIONS LEAGUE GROUP STAGES FOR THE FIRST TIME, BEGINNING WITH AN EPIC 3-2 VICTORY OVER BARCELONA

2001-02

ST JAMES' PARK HOSTED A WORLD CUP QUALIFIER, ENGLAND BEATING ALBANIA 2-0.

Monty's Quiz

What is the colour of our away strip this season?

2009 is the 40th Anniversary of winning the Fairs Cup (UEFA Cup), who scored in both legs to earn us that win?

Which two people have managed Blackburn Rovers, Newcastle and Liverpool?

In the popular rhyme, how many magpies does it take to get Silver?

If you got the bus from Gateshead for £1.85 to the match and at the match bought a Programme and a Pie at £3.00 each, then got the bus home... how much will you have spent?

Which ex Newcastle manager led England to the World Cup semi finals in 1990?

Who did Malcolm Macdonald score his first Newcastle United hat-trick against?

How many times have United won the FA Cup?

I'm sitting at St. James' Park and if I look directly forward I can see the top of the Tyne Bridge, which stand am I sitting in?

In a league if team A, wins 25 games and draws 5, scoring a total of 40 goals but conceding 25. And team B wins 21 games and draws 17 scoring a total of 27 goals but conceding 10... which team would finish in higher?

CREATING CHANCES

THE 2008/09 CREATING CHANCES PROGRAMME SAW MAGPIE STARS GETTING INVOLVED IN COMMUNITY PROJECTS THAT ARE SUPPORTED BY THE CLUB'S OFFICIAL CHARITY, THE NEWCASTLE UNITED FOUNDATION.

STEVEN TAYLOR, ANDY CARROLL AND DAVID EDGAR

HOSTING FUN FOOTBALL GAMES AND A POETRY READING CLASS AT CRUDDAS PARK LIBRARY, NEWCASTLE, AS PART OF THE READING STARS INITIATIVE THAT PROMOTES READING WITH YOUNGSTERS.

Steven Taylor said: "It's the second season I've been involved in the Creating Chances scheme and all of the lads enjoy putting something back into the community.

"It's a chance for us and the Club to help highlight the good work done by so many groups and charities in the North East."

SHOLA AMEOBI AND DAMIEN DUFF

HELPING OUT AT WHITEHOUSE FARM, NORTHUMBERLAND, ON A SCHOOL VISIT TO PROMOTE THE MATCH FIT INITIATIVE, WHICH ENCOURAGES HEALTHY EATING AND ACTIVE LIFESTYLES WITH SCHOOL CHILDREN IN THE EAST END OF NEWCASTLE.

The youngsters were given an educational tour, learning first hand about the food chain, bringing to life where healthy food comes from. The players were happy to answer questions from the children about their own healthy eating habits and pre-match fitness routines. They even joined in and helped the youngsters bath a pig.

Damien said: "Eating the right food is very important, not only for sports people but for everyone. It is nice for us to be able to pass on good advice about healthy eating."

JONAS GUTIERREZ AND JOSE ENRIQUE

LEARNING TO PLAY THE BOOMDANG DRUMS AT A WORKSHOP AT THE SAGE GATESHEAD, RUN BY THE KICKZ PERFECT PITCH PROJECT THAT INVITES YOUNG PEOPLE TO TAKE UP AN INTEREST IN MUSIC, FUNDED BY THE BRIT TRUST

Working in partnership with The Sage Gateshead, the Magpies' Perfect Pitch project teaches young people a wide range of musical genres and skills to Bronze Art award standard.The appearance of the two Newcastle United stars also coincided with the announcement of a major three-year donation to the Kickz programme by the BRIT Trust. And wing-king Jonas admits it's always nice to add another string to your bow, or rather beat to your drum.

"Now I will go home and tell my family that I can play the drums!

"It was good fun and both myself and Jose really enjoyed it. We practised for one hour and then played live in front of the people in the cafe and I think we were very good."

MICHAEL OWEN AND NICKY BUTT

HELPING OUT WITH GARDENING AND TEA-MAKING DUTIES AT THE LAWRENCE COURT CARE HOME IN BYKER, NEWCASTLE, ALONGSIDE YOUNG ADULTS FROM THE PRINCE'S TRUST TEAM PROGRAMME.

Owen and Butt donned gardening gloves and did their bit to brighten up the care home grounds and Nicky said: "It's always nice to meet people in the community, both young and old.

"It's been a good day and it's nice to be able to get out in the community. It's not every day we do things like this and hopefully it will benefit a few young people who haven't had the best of starts in life.

The Prince's Trust Team initiative is a 12 week self-development programme for unemployed young people generally from difficult backgrounds, perhaps young offenders, coming out of care or from a drug/alcohol dependent situation.

RYAN TAYLOR

TAKING PART IN A TABLE FOOTBALL CHALLENGE FOR THE TOMA FUND

Taylor visited Walbottle Campus in the city's West End to help raise the profile of the Toma Fund, the charity set up in memory of Jordan Thompson (aka Toma) who was a pupil at the school and a promising Newcastle United Academy player. And Tayls emerged triumphant as he picked up his first piece of silverware on Tyneside following a tense 5-4 victory in the final of the "Toma Table Football Challenge"

Ryan, who also handed out certificates to pupils with 100% attendance records, said: "It was great to come out to the school and meet the children. Some of them haven't missed a day of school for ten years and that is incredible. Credit to them and also to their parents because that's a fantastic achievement."

The Toma Fund received a £4,000 donation from the Creating Chances programme with the money being used to equip a music room at the Royal Victoria Infirmary in Newcastle for teenage cancer patients.

FAIRS CUP

IT WAS JUST OVER 40 YEARS AGO THAT NEWCASTLE UNITED WON THE INTER-CITIES FAIRS CUP ON THEIR FIRST FORAY INTO EUROPE, AND IN MAY 2009, UNITED HELD A CELEBRATORY DINNER AT ST. JAMES' PARK TO MARK THE OCCASION – THEY BEAT THE TOP HUNGARIAN SIDE OF THE DAY, UJPEST DOZSA, 6- 2 ON AGGREGATE IN THE TWO-LEGGED FINAL.

BACK IN THE 1960S, ONLY THE LEAGUE CHAMPIONS FROM EACH COUNTRY COMPETED IN THE EUROPEAN CUP (OR CHAMPIONS LEAGUE AS IT IS NOW) WHICH MEANT THE FAIRS CUP (NOW THE EUROPA LEAGUE) CONTAINED TEAMS FROM THE TOP ECHELONS OF EUROPE'S BEST LEAGUES. IF THAT WAS STILL THE CASE TODAY, MANCHESTER UNITED WOULD BE IN THE EUROPEAN CUP AND THE LIKES OF CHELSEA AND LIVERPOOL IN THE FAIRS CUP – SO THAT PUTS INTO PERSPECTIVE WHAT A FABULOUS ACHIEVEMENT IT WAS FOR UNITED TO HAVE LIFTED THE CUP.

The two pictures are a 'then and now', the famous team line-up with the Cup in 1969, and the picture taken at the Dinner 40 years on. Sadly manager Joe Harvey is no longer with us having passed away in 1989, but the rest of the squad remains intact, including Dane Benny Arentoft who scored in the second leg of the Final and travelled over to Newcastle from his homeland.

The Cup is the same though! It is held outright by Barcelona however the Catalan club agreed to let United have it 'back' for the duration of the 40-year celebrations so skipper Bob Moncur, and Alan Foggon, who also both scored in the second-leg of the Final, travelled over to the Nou Camp to bring it back to Tyneside once more.

NEWCASTLE UNITED

THEN AND NOW – THE SQUAD IN THEIR PLAYING DAYS ABOVE AND HERE, AT THE REUNION

TOP TEN GOALS 2008/9

IT MAY NOT HAVE BEEN A VINTAGE SEASON FOR NEWCASTLE UNITED, BUT THERE WERE STILL SOME MEMORABLE GOALS ALONG THE WAY. THEY ARE LISTED IN THE ORDER THEY WERE SCORED THROUGHOUT THE SEASON.

ANDY CARROLL CELEBRATES
HIS EQUALISER AT STOKE

OBA MARTINS v MAN UNITED A, 17/08/08

United's season off to a flying start at the home of the Champions, as five-foot seven-inch Martins leapt above Nemanja Vidić to head home Danny Guthrie's 22nd minute corner. Oba's opening day cracker was cancelled out by Darren Fletcher but Newcastle came away from Old Trafford with a very good point.

OBA MARTINS v ASTON VILLA H, 03/11/08

On the hour mark, Oba received the ball outside the box from Joey Barton, with his back to goal and two men around him. A split second later, he had swivelled and hit the ball with his left foot, along the ground and into the bottom corner. A fabulous, instinctive strike; no wonder he was doing somersaults after it.

OBA MARTINS v WIGAN H, 15/11/08

With the scores level late into the game, Charles N'Zogbia fed Martins on the left-hand angle of the box. The Nigerian controlled the ball with his first touch then, with virtually no backlift, hit an absolute thunderbolt which flew like a homing missile past the helpless – and motionless – Chris Kirkland.

DAMIEN DUFF NETS UNITED'S LAST MINUTE WINNER AGAINST TOTTENHAM

MICHAEL OWEN v PORTSMOUTH A, 14/12/08

The skipper led by example as The Magpies recorded their biggest win of the campaign. Jonás Gutiérrez supplied the through-ball after intercepting a loose Pompey pass and Owen, on his 29th birthday, arced the ball beautifully over the onrushing David James to give his side the lead.

DANNY GUTHRIE v PORTSMOUTH A, 14/12/08

In the final minute at Fratton Park, Habib Beye's lofted pass was flicked by Guthrie to Michael Owen. He played in Shola Ameobi who raced forward and pulled it back for Guthrie. The young midfielder had continued his run from the half way line and his first-time finish from just inside the box – his first for Newcastle – was a just reward.

DAMIEN DUFF v TOTTENHAM H, 21/12/08

Irish ace Duff had been on the pitch for just two minutes, and only 20 seconds of normal time remained when he brought the ball down, juggled it and played it into the feet of fellow sub Mark Viduka. The Aussie cleverly back-heeled it into Duff's path and he finished with an inch-perfect left-foot shot past Gomes into the far corner.

MICHAEL OWEN v WEST HAM H, 10/01/09

Although Owen is known more for his prowess in the penalty box than outside of it, this one came from the edge of the area. José Enrique rolled the ball to him in acres of space 25 yards out and, when Collins slipped, it was the cue for him to drill a powerful shot which took Robert Green by surprise.

STEVEN TAYLOR v HULL A, 14/03/09

Tayls started out as a striker at Whitley Bay Juniors, and you could see that striker's instinct from the way he clipped home this volleyed equaliser. Geremi took a throw-in deep inside the Hull half, Nicky Butt crossed it in from the right and centre-back Taylor finished with aplomb.

ANDY CARROLL v STOKE A, 11/04/09

Alan Shearer was seeking his first point as Newcastle manager and United were trailing 1-0 at the Britannia Stadium with nine minutes left. Then Damien Duff sent over a deep cross and local boy Carroll strained every muscle in his neck to generate enough power to send a tremendous towering header looping over the line.

STEVEN TAYLOR v MIDDLESBROUGH H, 11/05/09

The net nearly came off when Taylor's magnificent header from Danny Guthrie's right-wing corner hit it – and the roof of St. James' Park nearly came off with the noise as the fans celebrated. It lit the fuse for a 3-1 win which took United out of the bottom three – but sadly, they could not stay there.

PETER BEARDSLEY'S DREAM TEAM

PETER BEARDSLEY, A GENUINE NEWCASTLE LEGEND IN HIS TWO SPELLS WITH UNITED WHEN HE SCORED 119 GOALS IN 326 APPEARANCES FOR THE MAGPIES, HAS PLAYED WITH AND AGAINST THE VERY BEST THE WORLD OF FOOTBALL HAS TO OFFER.

THIS YEAR WE'VE TAPPED INTO HIS VAST INTERNATIONAL EXPERIENCE (REMEMBER HE WON 59 ENGLAND CAPS AND PLAYED A MAJOR PART IN ENGLAND REACHING THE SEMI-FINALS OF THE 1990 WORLD CUP) TO HEAR A SELECT X1 THAT HE CONSIDERS THE BEST FOOTBALLERS HE HAS HAD THE PRIVILEGE TO PLAY AGAINST AND ONE HE'D BE PROUD TO MANAGE! READ ON AND YOU'LL FIND OUT WHY.

PAOLO MALDINI

PETER SHILTON, GOALKEEPER

'Shilts' was by far and away the best keeper I've seen, an awesome presence between the posts. I only ever played with him for England but in league games when he was in the opposing goal, it would take a phenomenal strike to beat him. People tell me 1966 World Cup winner Gordon Banks was the best but for me, 'Shilts' had no equal.

ERIC GERETS, RIGHT BACK

Belgium may not be renowned as a major football nation but they produced a right back in the 1980s who was exceptional. A leader, superb defender and a vital cog supporting the frontmen. I never got much change out of him. Push it past him and he had the pace, try and out fox him and he'd be one step ahead of you. A rock in the back four.

PAOLO MALDINI, LEFT BACK

Paolo only retired at the end of last season, and played until he was 40! Can you believe that, unthinkable in today's fast and furious game. A one club man too (AC Milan), what I liked about him best was his coolness on the ball coupled with tremendous natural athleticism. I always thought he wouldn't be out of place in any position on the pitch, such was his natural talent.

FRANZ BECKENBAUER, CENTRE HALF

I played against 'The Kaiser' when he was with New York Cosmos in 1981 when I had a short spell with Vancouver Whitecaps playing in the North American Soccer League. He was widely recognised as the most influential player in German football and the best sweeper the game had ever seen – and even at 36 I could see why. I never saw him put a foot wrong, miss a tackle or send a pass astray. With an economy of effort he made the game look so simple.

DANIEL PASSARELLA, CENTRE HALF

World Cup skipper with Argentina in 1978, I came up against him in the NASL when he was with Tampa Bay Rowdies – and if ever there's been a tougher more uncompromising centre half, then I've yet to meet him. I'd make sure I would play down the flanks when we met, otherwise you could bet on being black and blue come the full time whistle. For all that though, you'd love to have him lining up with you.

BRYAN ROBSON, MIDFIELD

Universally known as Captain Marvel, he was a great help to me when I first joined the England set-up. Always offering advice and taking time to help his teammates he had a phenomenal 'engine', was a robust tackler and had a fabulous eye for goal. He would drive teams on through sheer enthusiasm and determination and possibly only Steven Gerrard in the modern game is someone who could be compared to the former England captain.

LOTHAR MATTHAUS, MIDFIELD

England might have won the World Cup in 1990 if it hadn't been for this man. Small in stature but a colossus on the field he was the driving force in Germany's midfield and inspired all those around him to raise their game. Efficient, quick of mind and feet, David Platt and Paul Gascoigne had to be at their absolute best to contain him. When you see he won an amazing 150 caps, it shows how long he managed to stay at the peak of his profession.

LOTHAR MATTHAUS

GEORGE BEST, STRIKER

Probably Britain's best footballer, and a tragic loss to the game when he passed away in 2005. I'd seen all his wonderful goals for Manchester United when I was growing up, I loved the one against Chelsea when he skipped through the defence at pace, avoiding lunge after lunge before brilliantly beating Peter Bonetti but he was humble and generous too. At Vancouver we played his team, San Jose Earthquakes and beat them 5 – 1. I hit a hat-trick and he came up to me afterwards to congratulate me. The funny thing was he thought I must have been a Canadian lad and couldn't believe it when I told him I was a Geordie!

GEORGE BEST

MARADONA, STRIKER

I came face to face with Maradona in the 1986 World Cup in Mexico when he scored the infamous 'hand of God goal'. Put that to one side though, the second he scored in that game, and everything else he did on the pitch that day marked him down as a football genius. My teammate Terry Butcher wouldn't shake hands with him after the game because he had cheated and although his reputation also suffered later in his career, he remains, in my view, second only to Pele in terms of being a pure footballing genius.

PELE, STRIKER

The best player the world has ever seen and one you'll never see the like of again. He was in his prime when I was a little lad growing up and learning my football so you can imagine what a thrill it was for me to be on the same pitch as the two-time World Cup winner. He could do everything with a ball and if you think Cristiano Ronaldo has quality, Pele would put him in the shade. Some of the football he played at the 1970 Mexico World Cup makes compulsive viewing.

MARCO VAN BASTEN, CENTRE FORWARD

Here was a centre forward with outstanding talent. We had a decent team at Euro 88 but when we came up against the Dutch, and after Bryan Robson gave us an early lead, they 'hammered' us 3 – 1, and van Basten got a hat-trick – all three goals being a master-class in the art of finishing. And do you remember the goal he got in the Final against Russia? One of the greatest strikes of all time as he hit a dipping volley from Arnold Muhren's deep cross past the Russian 'keeper from an acute angle – absolutely stunning.

MARCO VAN BASTEN

4x5 FILM

SXC

NEWCASTLE UNITED

SO HERE IS THE FULL PETER BEARDSLEY TEAM

PETER SHILTON	ENGLAND	125 CAPS
ERIC GERETS	BELGIUM	86 CAPS
PAOLO MALDINI	ITALY	126 CAPS
FRANZ BECKENBAUER	GERMANY	103 CAPS
DANIEL PASSARELLA	ARGENTINA	70 CAPS
BRYAN ROBSON	ENGLAND	90 CAPS
LOTHAR MATTHAUS	GERMANY	150 CAPS
GEORGE BEST	N IRELAND	37 CAPS
MARADONA	ARGENTINA	91 CAPS
PELE	BRAZIL	92 CAPS
MARCO VAN BASTEN	HOLLAND	58 CAPS

SPOT THE BALL!

LOOK CAREFULLY AT THE PICTURE ABOVE AND USING YOUR SKILL, TRY TO WORK OUT WHERE THE BALL MIGHT BE!

ANSWER PAGE 61

BLACK 'N' WHITE STRIPES

THE BLACK AND STRIPES OF NEWCASTLE UNITED ARE RENOWNED THE WORLD OVER. HERE WE TRACE THE ORIGINS OF UNITED'S FAMOUS COLOURS AND HOW THEY HAVE CHANGED THROUGH THE YEARS SINCE THE DAYS OF NEWCASTLE EAST END AT THE END OF THE 19TH CENTURY.

IT WAS WAY BACK ON AUGUST 2ND, 1894, WHEN THE MAGPIES DECIDED TO DISCARD THE RED OF UNITED'S FOUNDING CLUB, NEWCASTLE EAST END HAVING PULLED ON ALL RED SHIRTS THEN, AS WELL AS A JERSEY OF, AMAZINGLY, RED AND WHITE STRIPES!

The Club's board meeting journal records the change in colours: 'It was agreed that the Club's colours should be changed from red shirts and white knickers to black and white shirts (two-inch stripe) and dark knickers.

This would stop the frequent colour clashes which were occurring in the Football League's second tier at the time. Nowhere, though does it state why they selected black and white, which were the same colours as the Northumberland county side. And there is still no definitive answer to that mystery!

A few theories have been put forward over time. The most popular surrounds a fervent supporter from the city's Blackfriars monastery, Father Dalmatius Houtmann. The Dutchman was often to be seen with United's players in the years before the turn of the century, the monastery being just a goal-kick away from St. James' Park. He was dressed in a traditional black and white habit, and it has been suggested that the Club decided to adopt his colours.

Another legend that has been handed down over the years is the story of a pair of magpies nesting in the old Victorian Stand at St. James' Park. It was said that United's players of the time became so attached to the two birds that they picked their distinctive colours of black and white and named themselves the Magpies.

Finally, there is a suggestion that goes back deep into history to the time of the English Civil War and a famous 17th-century Cavalier, William Cavendish (1593-1676). As Earl, and, later, Duke of Newcastle, he had strong connections with Tyneside and Northumberland. The Cavendish heraldic crest of three white stags on a black background – the first black'n'white connection – was to be seen all over the North-East.

And when Civil War raged, Cavendish raised a volunteer army on Tyneside, known as the Newcastle Whitecoats, and their black and white attire became very distinctive – probably the very first Toon Army!

In the early years of the 20th century, roughly 100 years ago, United pulled on a shirt with broad stripes featured on the front and back of the jersey. It was the start of a remarkable series of differing designs of black and white stripes.

In the Twenties the stripes became narrower, while centre stripes varied from white to black. Generally, though, the Club shirt remained the same right up to season 1958-59 with the exception of a change in collar from the "grand-dad" look to a conventional one.

However, with Charlie Mitten installed as boss, his modern and continental influence gave the black'n'white a dramatic change. In came a streamlined version, but few liked it in an era of traditional values.

The kit was perhaps a decade ahead of its time and was rapidly shelved, to be replaced by a more conventional style for the Sixties. It was rare for the club to show any crest on the shirt up to then, apart from in FA Cup Finals.

During the following decade, kit manufacturers started to play a major part in football. A succession of companies like Bukta, Umbro and Asics started to find imaginative ways of designing United's classical black'n'white striped shirt using logos, side flashes, different styles of collars, and the introduction of blue tints as United's third colour.

And with the introduction of a Club sponsor, the Magpies had Newcastle Breweries' famous Blue Star emblazoned on the shirt from season 1982-83, replaced by new sponsors Greenalls, then NTL's colourful logo and afterwards the distinctive Northern Rock banner.

Season 1989-90 saw probably the most unusual design when a mix of narrow and broad black and white stripes produced a "bar-code" look that took a while to get used to.

WORLD GIANTS ADIDAS HAVE BEEN UNITED'S KIT MANUFACTURER AS WELL AS OFFICIAL SPONSOR SINCE THE MID 1990S AND THEY HAVE PRODUCED A SUCCESSION OF QUALITY DESIGNED KITS.

IT IS QUITE AMAZING WHAT CAN BE DONE WITH BLACK AND WHITE STRIPES!

SEASON STATISTICS 2008/09

	LEAGUE	FA CUP	LEG CUP	2008/09	TOTAL NUFC
SHOLA AMEOBI	14 (8) 4	0 (0) 0	0 (0) 0	14 (8) 4	149 (103) 50
JOEY BARTON	6 (3) 1	0 (0) 0	0 (0) 0	6 (3) 1	26 (6) 2
SEBASTIEN BASSONG	26 (4) 0	2 (0) 0	2 (0) 0	30 (4) 0	30 (4) 0
HABIB BEYE	22 (1) 0	0 (0) 0	1 (0) 0	23 (1) 0	51 (3) 0
NICKY BUTT	33 (0) 0	2 (0) 0	2 (0) 0	37 (0) 0	139 (12) 5
CACAPA	4 (2) 0	0 (0) 0	1 (0) 0	5 (2) 0	24 (5) 2
ANDREW CARROLL	5 (9) 3	1 (1) 0	0 (0) 0	6 (10) 3	7 (22) 3
FABRICIO COLOCCINI	34 (0) 0	2 (0) 0	2 (0) 0	38 (0) 0	38 (0) 0
DAMIEN DUFF	28 (2) 3	2 (0) 0	1 (0) 0	31 (2) 3	75 (10) 5
DAVID EDGAR	7 (4) 1	1 (0) 0	0 (1) 0	8 (5) 1	13 (10) 2
JOSE ENRIQUE	24 (2) 0	1 (0) 0	1 (0) 0	26 (2) 0	49 (7) 0
GEREMI	11 (4) 0	0 (0) 0	2 (0) 0	13 (4) 0	38 (7) 1
SHAY GIVEN	22 (0) 0	2 (0) 0	2 (0) 0	26 (0) 0	462 (1) 0
IGNACIO GONZALES	0 (2) 0	0 (0) 0	0 (0) 0	0 (2) 0	0 (2) 0
DANNY GUTHRIE	21 (3) 2	2 (0) 0	1 (0) 0	24 (3) 2	24 (3) 2
JONAS GUTIERREZ	23 (7) 0	1 (1) 0	1 (0) 0	25 (8) 0	25 (8) 0
STEVE HARPER	16 (0) 0	0 (0) 0	0 (0) 0	16 (0) 0	117 (10) 0
PETER LOVENKRANDS	8 (4) 3	0 (0) 0	0 (0) 0	8 (4) 3	8 (4) 3
KAZENGA LUALUA	0 (3) 0	0 (1) 0	0 (0) 0	0 (4) 0	0 (9) 0
OBAFEMI MARTINS	21 93) 8	0 (0) 0	1 (0) 0	22 (3) 8	89 (15) 35
JAMES MILNER	2 (0) 0	0 (0) 0	1 (0) 1	3 (0) 1	100 (36) 11
KEVIN NOLAN	10 (1) 0	0 (0) 0	0 (0) 0	10 (1) 0	10 (1) 0
CHARLES N'ZOGBIA	14 (4) 1	2 (0) 0	2 (0) 1	18 (4) 2	114 (4) 11
MICHAEL OWEN	21 (7) 8	2 (0) 0	1 (1) 2	24 (8) 10	65 (14) 30
ALAN SMITH	4 (2) 0	0 (0) 0	0 (0) 0	4 (2) 0	34 (9) 0
RYAN TAYLOR	8 (2) 0	0 (0) 0	0 (0) 0	8 (2) 0	8 (2) 0
STEVEN TAYLOR	25 (2) 4	1 (0) 0	1 (0) 0	27 (2) 4	139 (11) 9
MARK VIDUKA	6 (60) 0	0 (0) 0	0 (0) 0	6 (6) 0	27 (13) 7
XISCO	3 (2) 1	1 (0) 0	0 (1) 0	4 (3) 1	4 (3) 1

QUIZ 1. PAGE 14

1 OBA MARTINS (V MAN UTD) AND PETER LOVENKRANDS (V MIDDLESBROUGH)
2 TOTTENHAM HOTSPUR
3 CRAIG BELLAMY
4 LIVERPOOL
5 DONCASTER ROVERS
6 SHOLA AMEOBI
7 WEST BROMWICH ALBION
8 KC STADIUM (HULL CITY)
9 KEVIN NOLAN
10 RYAN TAYLOR

QUIZ 2. PAGE 27

1 2000 (FA CUP SEMI FINAL V CHELSEA)
2 BOB MONCUR
3 MANCHESTER CITY
4 SUNDERLAND
5 PETER BEARDSLEY. PAUL GASCOIGNE, STUART PEARCE, CHRIS WADDLE
6 JACKIE MILBURN
7 READING
8 SOUTHAMPTON AND BLACKBURN
9 DAVID EDGAR (SON OF EDDIE)
10 PAVEL SRNICEK AND SHAKA HISLOP

WORD SEARCH. PAGE 38

BEARDSLEY	ADAMS
BERESFORD	BERGKAMP
FERDINAND	CANTONA
GINOLA	DROGBA
HARPER	HENRY
JENAS	JAMES
SOLANO	KEANE
SPEED	ROONEY
TAYLOR	TORRES
WOODGATE	ZOLA

SPOT THE BALL. PAGE 57

2009/10 COCA-COLA CHAMPIONSHIP FIXTURES

DATE	OPPOSITION	H/A	K-OFF	SCORE
SAT 08 AUGUST	WEST BROM	A	5:30	
SAT 15 AUGUST	READING	H	5:20	
WED 19 AUGUST	SHEFFIELD WEDNESDAY	H	7:45	
SAT 22 AUGUST	CRYSTAL PALACE	A	3:00	
MON 31 AUGUST	LEICESTER CITY	H	7:45	
SUN 13 SEPTEMBER	CARDIFF CITY	A	2:05	
WED 16 SEPTEMBER	BLACKPOOL	A	7:45	
SAT 19 SEPTEMBER	PLYMOUTH ARGYLE	H	3:00	
SAT 26 SEPTEMBER	IPSWICH TOWN	A	5:30	
WED 30 SEPTEMBER	QUEENS PARK RANGERS	H	7:45	
SAT 03 OCTOBER	BRISTOL CITY	H	3:00	
SAT 17 OCTOBER	NOTTINGHAM FOREST	A	5:20	
TUE 20 OCTOBER	SCUNTHORPE UNITED	A	7:45	
SAT 24 OCTOBER	DONCASTER ROVERS	H	3:00	
MON 02 NOVEMBER	SHEFFIELD UNITED	A	7:45	
SAT 07 NOVEMBER	PETERBOROUGH UNITED	H	3:00	
SAT 21 NOVEMBER	PRESTON NORTH END	A	3:00	
SAT 28 NOVEMBER	SWANSEA CITY	H	3:00	
SAT 05 DECEMBER	WATFORD	H	3:00	
TUE 08 DECEMBER	COVENTRY CITY	A	7:45	
SAT 12 DECEMBER	BARNSLEY	A	3:00	
SAT 19 DECEMBER	MIDDLESBROUGH	H	3:00	
SAT 26 DECEMBER	SHEFFIELD WEDNESDAY	A	3:00	
MON 28 DECEMBER	DERBY COUNTY	H	3:00	
SAT 09 JANUARY	READING	A	3:00	
SAT 16 JANUARY	WEST BROM	H	3:00	
WED 27 JANUARY	CRYSTAL PALACE	H	7:45	
SAT 30 JANUARY	LEICESTER CITY	A	3:00	
SAT 06 FEBRUARY	CARDIFF CITY	H	3:00	
TUE 09 FEBRUARY	DERBY COUNTY	A	7:45	
SAT 13 FEBRUARY	SWANSEA CITY	A	3:00	
WED 17 FEBRUARY	COVENTRY CITY	H	7:45	
SAT 20 FEBRUARY	PRESTON NORTH END	H	3:00	
SAT 27 FEBRUARY	WATFORD	A	3:00	
SAT 06 MARCH	BARNSLEY	H	3:00	
SAT 13 MARCH	MIDDLESBROUGH	A	3:00	
WED 17 MARCH	SCUNTHORPE UNITED	H	3:00	
SAT 20 MARCH	BRISTOL CITY	A	3:00	
TUE 23 MARCH	DONCASTER ROVERS	A	7:45	
SAT 27 MARCH	NOTTINGHAM FOREST	H	3:00	
SAT 03 APRIL	PETERBOROUGH UNITED	A	3:00	
MON 05 APRIL	SHEFFIELD UNITED	H	3:00	
SAT 10 APRIL	BLACKPOOL	H	3:00	
SAT 17 APRIL	PLYMOUTH ARGYLE	A	3:00	
SAT 24 APRIL	IPSWICH TOWN	H	3:00	
SUN 02 MAY	QUEENS PARK RANGERS	A	3:00	